PRAISE FOR
AN ECOLOGY OF GRATITUDE

"This fine book concerns two of my favourite subjects—writing and gratitude. Widmer-Carson combines research and her own experience to explore one of our most important sources of joy, generators of compassion and coping mechanisms. *An Ecology of Gratitude* will motivate and energize its readers to pick up a pen and start writing."
— Mary Pipher, author of *Women Rowing North* and *Letters to a Young Therapist*   www.marypipher.com

"I love this book and can't wait to spend 30 days (at least) with it, journaling on the rich and inspiring prompts that Lorraine Widmer-Carson maps out. Full of meaningful personal stories and heartfelt experiences, this book weaves together important research and time-sensitive concepts, with powerful writing prompts, bringing the practice of gratitude fully alive in a transformative way. A beautiful, practical, and deeply enriching read!"
— Aileen Gibb, master coach, author and inspirer of new conversations on life and leadership   www.aileengibb.com

"*An Ecology of Gratitude* associates the concepts of interaction and interdependence, fundamental to the science of ecology, with the recognition that our lives are nurtured by interactions and interdependencies with others. Widmer-Carson's suggested path towards a practice of gratitude has the potential to dramatically help readers make a much-needed mental shift from that of conquest and struggle to attitudes of appreciation and respect towards the living world."
— Jean-Louis Martin, senior scientist, emeritus, Centre for Functional and Evolutionary Ecology, Montpellier, France

"Widmer-Carson's focus on gratitude is such an important message for today's world. She gives many examples of the 'ripples that a good gratitude practice can generate'. How very true! *An Ecology of Gratitude* will motivate you to understand the waters you are swimming in and decide how to make your own ripples."
— Colleen Kelly, co-author of *The Abundant Not-for-Profit*

"We should all start our day with a page out of this book. *An Ecology of Gratitude* is one-part lived experience, and one-part encouragement to stretch our gratitude muscles. Widmer-Carson uses research, personal anecdotes, and plain positive energy to convince us of the benefits of writing in a journal and of the power of the pen."
— Corrie DiManno, Mayor of Banff (Alberta, Canada)

"Placing gratitude at the centre of our interactions—amongst family, at work, in community—seems like such a natural choice even if it is infrequently chosen. Widmer-Carson helps us all to tip the scales so that we choose gratitude more often, with intention and an understanding of how this can lift up our lives, our relationships, and our contributions. What a wonderful gift!"
— Ian Bird, chair, Global Fund for Community Foundations

"Gratitude sits there quietly, its magnitude often overlooked. To engage deeply with it, is like coming home to a human experience with profound connection to life around us. This book is full of encouragement to wake up and pay attention to the beauty that surrounds us, each and every day."
— Karina Birch, CEO and owner, Rocky Mountain Soap Company

An ECOLOGY *of* GRATITUDE

WRITING YOUR WAY
TO WHAT MATTERS

#grassrootsgratitude.ca
Know it. Show it. Grow it!

Lorraine Widmer-Carson

LORRAINE WIDMER-CARSON

For permissions contact: lorraine@grassrootsgratitude.ca.

An Ecology of Gratitude: Writing Your Way to What Matters
by Lorraine Widmer-Carson

Published by Lorraine Widmer-Carson

P.O. Box 1103
Banff, Alberta, T1L 1B1
Canada

ISBN: 978-1-7777785-0-7 (Paperback Book)
ISBN: 978-1-7777785-1-4 (Electronic Book)

Key words: Journal Practice. Writing. Habits of Mind. Gratitude. Kindness. Social Capital. Personal Growth.

Printed in Canada

First Edition

Book Design and Cover: Lieve Maas, brightlightgraphics.com
Editor: Dave Jarecki, davejarecki.com
Author Photo Credit: Lindsey Hill @ej.lifestyle

Every effort has been made to reference others respectfully and accurately.

For information about special discounts available for bulk purchases, philanthropic promotions, fund-raising, and educational needs, contact the author: lorraine@grassrootsgratitude.ca.

For more information about the author, kindness cookie recipe, and the author's reading list, visit: www.grassrootsgratitude.ca.

"I am not interested in weapons, whether words or guns. I want to be part of the rescue team for our tired, overcrowded planet. The rescuers will be those people who help other people to think clearly, to be honest and open-minded. They will be an anti-dote to those people who disconnect us. They will de-objectify, rehumanize, and make others more understandable and sympathetic. They will help create what philosopher Martin Buber called I-thou relationships for the human race."

Mary Pipher, from **Writing to Change the World**

DEDICATION

The profound gratitude I feel for my family, friends, peers and colleagues, past and present, is the anchor to each of my thoughts and stories shared in this book. Specifically, this book is dedicated to my families.

To my birth family: my mother, Dorothy (Dora) Esther Carson (née Guthrie, 1924 - 2002); my father, James Hilton Carson, M.D. (1923 - 1996); and my two sisters, Shirley Margaret and Donna Marie. I am proud to say that I come from a family of stubborn teachers, farmers and doctors. From these strong and secure seeds, I learned to take risks, make mistakes and stay confident that when I fell, my foundational support network would prop me up, patch me together and push me out the door again.

To Erwin, my husband, and our children, Philip, Matthew, Angela and Heidi: thank you all for the privilege of sharing this journey. Stronger, wiser, older and still a unit, we have made some excellent choices, taken risks and lost a few chips. During times when we faced disappointment and worst-case outcomes, our family glue held us together. We are bound by joy and love, and continue to use our stubborn persistence as good grist.

To my families of friends and fellow travellers: thank you for helping me pay attention, and for reminding me to keep my big rocks in the jar, my heart in my chest, my head on my shoulders and my feet on the ground (most of the time) as I continue to seek and honour what matters most.

ACKNOWLEDGING THE LAND

I wake up, walk, talk with my family and friends, tell stories, hike and ski within the Treaty 7 region of southern Alberta. With humility and deep respect, I acknowledge the past, the present and the future with our Indigenous relations in this place, my adopted home along the Bow River in the Canadian Rockies, commonly known as Banff National Park.

I wish to acknowledge the signatories to the southern Alberta Treaty 7 of 1877: the First Peoples from the Siksika, Kainai and Piikani of the Blackfoot Confederacy; the Tsuut'ina First Nations; the Stoney Nakoda Nations of Chiniki, Wesley and Bearspaw. This region is also home to the Métis Nation of Alberta, Region 3. I also wish to acknowledge the longstanding and continuing relations on either side of the Rockies since time immemorial of the Mountain Cree clan of Peechee, the Dene, the Ktunaxa and Secwépewmc Peoples. As a Treaty resident, I am working towards truth and reconciliation by aspiring to live in right relations with the people, flora, fauna, land, wind and waters of this place that I call home.

CONTENTS

A PRIMER ABOUT YOUR
GRATITUDE WRITING HABIT

Gratitude is like a corkscrew that touches our hearts and souls. It is also a hinge to the world beyond, connecting our soft spots to the larger universe. Through gratitude, we can look deeper inside ourselves, and simultaneously see our place within the greater ecosystem of systems beyond.

When approached on a regular basis, gratitude deepens our joys and brightens our burdens. And, as science makes clear, one of the most powerful ways to build our gratitude muscles is to write from a private place with a mindset of gratitude.[1]

They say that it takes at least 30 uncomfortable days to form a new habit, and that we may not notice any shifts until day 14 at the earliest. The book in your hands provides you with 30 days of suggestions for approaching, exploring and delving into your reasons for feeling grateful—with the help of pen (or pencil) and a bound journal.

By dedicating time and attention to building a regular writing habit, and by sowing, tilling and nurturing your reasons for being grateful, you can find ways to become happier and healthier in your life, and even grow into a more caring and purposeful human *bean*. Yes…a human bean, making full use of the potential and greatness inside of you (similar to Jack's famous beanstalk).

Through the habit of gratitude writing, and keeping a running tally of your gifts, joys, and even your burdens, you can flourish and stand taller in the world. But, fair warning: writing takes discipline, and being grateful demands courage, as it will bring you closer to tender places and vulnerabilities that you might rather keep buried in the soil.

In the end, what you'll discover is that once your gratitudes start sprouting, they will become a social contagion and demand action. As you pay attention, write notes and define important things happening in your life, I am certain you will find ideas on how to make your world a better place in which to live, work and play—one that will help all parts of your personal ecosystem flourish and thrive.

Primer Notes

[1] A number of books that discuss the science of gratitude helped with the writing of this book. A few of my favourites include the following: *The Little Book of Gratitude: Create a Life of Happiness and Wellbeing by Giving Thanks* (Robert A. Emmons, London, Great Britain: Octopus Publishing Group Ltd., 2016); *Thanks! How Practicing Gratitude Can Make You Happier* (Robert A. Emmons, New York, New York, Houghton Mifflin Harcourt Publishing Company, 2007); and *The Gratitude Project: How the Science of Thankfulness Can Rewire Our Brains for Resilience, Optimism and the Greater Good* (Jeremy Adam Smith, Kira M. Newman, Jason Marsh, and Dacher Keltner [eds], Oakland, California, New Harbinger Publications Inc. 2020). You can find a more extensive reading list on my website: wwwgrassrootsgratitude.ca.

INTRODUCTION

Gratitude is more than a greeting card sentiment. It is a compass, a mirror, and a personal calibration tool for viewing life with a richer perspective. Gratitude stems from a system of beliefs and attitudes that we hold about ourselves, others and the universe. Further, gratitude defines our essential matters and core values, and can help us flourish in an environment of gentle acceptance, hope and grace.

Your preferences, reactions, conversations and interactions quite likely contain hints of gratitude already. Your ways of expressing or recognizing gratitude may be culture-specific and normal in your world. However, by looking more carefully, labelling gratitude with greater insight and precision, and by applying the lens of gratitude to your daily contemplations, you will find more reasons to be hopeful, optimistic and motivated to take your next best step.

Gratitude creates its own force field, and can generate a reciprocal flow of energy. By giving and receiving, accepting gifts in the spirit intended, and reallocating your giving energy with intentional kindness, you can influence the dynamics of relationships at home and at work, and most importantly, in your relationship with yourself.

***

In 1992, I drove away from my home in Banff National Park, a valley that was once covered by a shallow inland sea, and headed eastward across the Canadian prairies. I left my four young children and husband at home, along with lists of routines, likes, preferences, habits, aversions, and a handful of emergency contact numbers just in case. I was on my way to a writing pilgrimage that would jumpstart the writing journey I continue to follow.

The Bow River Valley, my chosen home, is part of a montane ecosystem in the Canadian Rockies, with a geologic timeline of between 60 and 100 million years. The human history of this valley starts its record about 12,000 years ago, after the glaciers retreated. Ecologically speaking, it's a landscape that ranges from low lying wetlands with hot springs and excellent bird habitat, to harsh rocky peaks, high alpine lakes, and glaciers that feed the headwaters of the Lake Winnipeg Watershed. My neighbours and I go about our daily lives knowing that forces of nature are cyclical, and that fires, avalanches, summer snowstorms, mudslides and floods are possible occurrences. We know that Indigenous peoples have visited these lands for thousands of years prior to today, and that for eons, people have been using this landscape as a place for meeting, trading, foraging, hunting, gathering, and, of tremendous importance, for deep healing and spiritual quests.

As residents of this remarkable corner of the world, we need to accept our significant responsibilities, and are learning that every choice we make can profoundly impact our environmental, cultural, spiritual, recreational and economic lifelines. Living inside a national park, we must carefully manage ourselves, knowing that we share our natural corridors with bears, elk, deer, snails, and cougars to name a few, as well as travellers who arrive from all corners of the globe. We live in a place that is called "critical habitat," and our diverse human systems are very much a part of this complicated, wondrous mix of critical life-supporting variables.

Here, ecology readily comes to mind—the ecology of the place I call home, as well as the greater meaning of the word. Whether the system in question is natural, social or personal, every ecology is the study of relationships and the flow of energy. What I began to muse on during my drive, and continue to consider every day, is how gratitude informs our habits, and serves as an essential driver in our emotional ecology. It is very much like sunlight and oxygen—it energizes us, and helps us put down roots, finding our solid ground. Gratitude connects the dots between the causes we care about, and helps us identify our core beliefs and values.

***

From my earliest days as a young mother, I knew that I needed to spend time alone with my pens, journals and books in order to become a more self-aware and empathetic parent, daughter, wife, sister, friend, colleague and person. Since shifting my writing habit toward gratitude, I have been able to cope with more grace, grow with more humility, become more considerate of others and meet the demands of life in ways that I had never imagined.

In the context of recent geological history—just a tiny blip on the planet's timeline—our four children have grown into caring, responsible and inspirational adults. When our youngest, Heidi, started kindergarten, I expanded my worksite beyond the home, as an environmental educator, community grant-maker, fund-raiser, community facilitator and advocate for all things local. My broad range of interests culminated with the privilege of leading The Banff Canmore Community Foundation for 12 years.

I found that balancing our collective goals as a family and my personal goals as a community educator became easier when I disciplined myself to write every single morning. Three pages each day helped me *get my head on straight* before dashing into the kitchen to serve oatmeal, pack lunches and hurry the children out the door.

When I left my job at the foundation in 2017, I thought I would continue to support the local philanthropic sector in some way. Two years later, I received a message from the local high school's science teacher, inviting me to speak at the upcoming Honour Roll Society. Her note arrived out of the blue, and shared the following:

> *Our theme this year is about grit, perseverance, caring and giving back. I don't think there is anything grittier than the perseverance your kids have gone through with sports, having setbacks, then getting back up and keeping at it. I also thought it might be fun for the students to know about the person behind the community foundation and all the activities, programs and ways you have supported our school over the years. Regardless, I just wanted to let you know that you have really made a big impact on the school and the kids, and I thought it would be nice for them to put a face to the support you have given us.*

A committed and caring educator was asking me to speak to the topics of *grit, perseverance, setbacks, caring* and *giving back.* More than just being an invitation to speak, I saw her words as a snapshot of how our family was perceived in the community, and a heartwarming expression of genuine gratitude. I didn't call it a *gratitude letter* at the time, but today I can confidently label it as such.

After the event, I travelled to England on a writing retreat to deepen my understanding of the genre of life writing—the recording of memories and experiences. With distance, inspiration and time to process my thoughts, I returned to Canada, ready to commit to my study of gratitude, filtered through my life experiences—my personal journey for "ground-truthing" the science.

By researching and practicing gratitude, I have learned to take an inventory of my life. One thing I've discovered is that I likely undervalued gratitude during my younger days, because it was easily and readily available to me. I am lucky, and aware of my privileges. In fact, I have often introduced myself as *Lucky Lorrie*. However, in moments when I wasn't feeling lucky, I learned to keep writing, be humble, stay patient and wait. If I knew then what I know now, I might have spent more time savouring the good things, and launched more of my writing exercises by being grateful first, grumpy second.

As I have come to recognize, and as you may already know, it's easier to write about negatives and pains than it is to write about joys and gratitudes. I can't help but wonder how my life might be different today if I had started using gratitude as the primary filter to my thoughts earlier. Would I have been able to act on big decisions with more clarity and less anxiety? Would I have gained back the hours I spent ruminating on worries that never came to pass? If I had put more gratitude into my pen, would I have been able to energize my village with more confidence, optimism and trust? Can gratitude help you create more powerful and meaningful connections? I believe that the answer waiting for you to discover for yourself is a resounding "Yes!"

***

All these years later, my journal remains my faithful travelling companion. In fact, my writing continues to ground my morning ritual. My bookshelf is lined with more than 150 journals, representing my private way for witnessing changes in myself, my family and my community, as well as documenting the shifting sands of our world. I don't re-read the pages in the hopes of finding accuracy or reality. They provide temporal-spatial-emotional insight to confusion that exists along pathways of indecision; they are records of my ongoing attempt to seek clarity, establish boundaries, and define my personal priorities.

Now, I believe it's time to pay this awareness forward, and encourage readers such as yourself to try your hand at writing your way to what matters most. My motivation is to help you feel good about yourself, find new meaning, get unstuck, and grow in your professional, personal and life pursuits. By slowing down and taking stock of all of your reasons to be grateful, you can become more hopeful, optimistic, cheerful and trusting. A consistent writing practice will help you monitor life's circumstances, and benchmark your progress as you move forward or backward, or take care of yourself while stagnating in neutral.

When you pay deeper attention to the life that surrounds you through the lens of "Things that really matter," or "Things that are going well," you will find new reasons to frame your ideas and beliefs with greater empathy, kindness and grace. Most importantly, your gratitude writing practice will help you survey the ecology of your life, your village and your world with a new outlook. Venturing through this book's anecdotes and practices will help nudge your perspective in the direction of more life-affirming and positive habits of mind.

A gratitude writing practice can help you find balance in the midst of your personal ecosystems, as you acknowledge and accept the complexities and contradictions of everyday living. Even when change is constant, and worlds simultaneously contract and expand, taking 20 minutes to write in your journal will prove to be a clarifying and gratifying navigational tool.

By writing daily and mindfully, exploring the full range of your emotions, and intentionally looking for *the good stuff*, you will find yourself feeling less lonesome, more connected, and more aware of all the ways the world is working in your favour. With a mindset grounded in gratitude, your writing practice has the potential to inspire feelings that are revelatory and transformative.

When you write in a journal and track your gratitudes, your worries recede, joys advance, and a softening happens in places that may be physical, social, emotional or spiritual. With pen (or pencil) and paper, you will find time to pause, savour, reflect and pay attention to your heart, mind and energy. In so doing, you may become aware of memories you're holding back—or that may be holding YOU back—as well as goals that push you forward. As you write through your emotions, beliefs and insights, you will find yourself channelling your best efforts every day—physically, socially, emotionally and spiritually.

***

Since early in 2020, COVID-19 has shown us just how much our understanding of the world has shifted. I believe gratitude is the key to recalibrating our moral compasses, and I don't come to this assessment by whim. I have dedicated the last 30 years of my life to a personal writing practice that helped me find meaning and purpose, grow in my understanding of science and systems, and see gratitude as an answer to our social, environmental, political, economic and civic engagement issues.

Have you ever heard of the Precautionary Principle?[2] I was first introduced to this idea when I joined the Banff-Bow Valley Study, a public participation process. The idea is related to assessing risk and being prudent. It contains an element of social responsibility, and is a way to check yourself as wild and crazy ideas float into your mind. A journal entry from 1996 cites it in the voice of process mediator and lawyer, Craig Darling:

> *If you act as if it doesn't matter and it doesn't matter,*
> *Then it doesn't matter.*
> *BUT*
> *If you act as if it doesn't matter and it matters?*
> *Then it matters.*

In the journey of my life, I have spent a great deal of time trying to figure out what really matters; what my first priorities are; what fears, worries and immaturities I can release. In 2020, I found that all of the new fears, worries and uncertainties about COVID began compounding atop previous concerns. Today, as the virus continues to mutate and shape-shift like every good demon, people remain skeptical and cynical, and the rifts between us continue to rise. Like many, I have done my best to cope with too many ideas, too much information, and competing demands on my priorities. By maintaining my writing practice, I am able to ask myself three essential clarifying questions every morning:

- What am I thinking now?
- What might I be missing?
- What are the things that really matter?

Helping you ask and answer these same questions for yourself is truly what this book is about. By writing honestly with pen and paper, you will discover, unbundle and remind yourself about the things that *really matter* in your life as you make your way to what's next. With insight, hindsight and vision, you will start to see through your mind's eye; much like the fox says in *The Little Prince*, "And now here is my secret, a very simple secret: It is only with the heart that one can see rightly; what is essential is invisible to the eye."[3]

In the weeks to come, writing will help you define the invisible filters to your thoughts, and your reasons to move forward with greater optimism, confidence and gratitude. By writing your way to gratitude, you will be amazed at the cast of characters who show up on the page—some encouraging you along, others obstructing your path. You will be humbled with the realization that things may actually be working out better than you thought. By quieting your negative and cynical voices, you will find more joy in your stories, remember other things that matter, and realize that a larger system of people, places and networks are supporting you. You will find a new way to see the ecology of your own life.

As you embark, enjoy taking stock of small moments that bring you energy and hope, that offer glimmers of grace, and that illuminate your reasons to be grateful. The invitation is for you to sit quietly and enjoy the solitude as you breathe, write, imagine, reflect, remember and look forward.

With encouragement, you will gain greater insights into your life circumstances, understand others with greater empathy, and quiet your contemplations with calm and simplicity. With pen, paper and personal space, may you rediscover your personal wellspring of joy and gratitude.

Throughout the book:

- I will urge you to write in a journal. As you do, you may choose to write letters, make lists, take photos, or sketch diagrams. If you are averse to the physical act of writing, or cannot write for one reason or another, consider using voice-to-text to participate in your own journey. Whatever you choose, be sure to pay attention, stay kind and be gentle with yourself.
- I will cite science as an influential motivator and proof point for the work you are doing.
- I will remind you that writing can help you be a curious visitor and travelling companion in the story of your life.
- And, I will share anecdotes that point to a deeply personal truth of my own: that if I had understood the power of gratitude earlier in my life, and seen it as a critical link to pro-social behaviour, I would have had much greater insight into my work, and an even greater conviction for the power of community philanthropy.

By helping to infuse your writing with gratitude, my hope is that you are motivated to energize your efforts and help make your village a kinder, smarter and more caring place—locally, regionally, nationally and globally.

BEFORE YOU BEGIN

After years of doing good work with good people at the community level, my journal practice demands that I keep paying attention, looking ahead and making a conscious effort to seek out essential truths from among the daily swirl of information, emotions and expectations. The more I learn, the more I am convinced that gratitude is one of our highest powers and strongest muscles, and that practicing gratitude requires focused attention and intentional training.

This book is my attempt to distill the essence of my personal ecology based on sound scientific insights that others have offered. It is a thought exercise by which I seek to simplify contradictions and complexities based on the life I have been living, according to some of the books I have read, and the influence of internal and external forces that are alive in the world.

In the book's back pages, you will find a few tools that will assist you on your journey and help you to benchmark your success:

- The first, a gratitude gauge, is a quiz that asks you to gauge your gratitude. Take this quiz before you begin, to help benchmark your starting point (page 182).
- The second, the gratitude accountability list, is a personal accountability tool that you will complete on your eighth day of gratitude journaling. There's no harm in glancing at it now, but wait until Day 8 to fill it out (page 184).
- The third, which corresponds with Day 23, invites you to explore the compass points that guide your life, and add some soul to your personal values (page 188).

Please know that this book is not meant to *force* you into following a prescriptive type of practice. While each chapter's title includes the word *Day* (Day 1, Day 2, etc.), by no means do you have to approach these practices every day over consecutive days. As you find a rhythm, you may wish to approach only one or two practices a week, and spread your journey out over multiple months. The goal is to commit to a practice that suits you, not one that forces you to wrap up or finish in a certain amount of time. With that said, I do encourage you to follow the practices in the order in which they appear, as many of them feed into messages that come later.

Finally, if you find places where I have misrepresented any science, or someone's role in a story, it is an honest mistake. If you find an error or discrepancy that you would like to discuss, or if you have a question or inspiration to share, please write a note to yourself first, and to me second.

CUSTOMIZING YOUR PERSONAL PRACTICE

If you've come this far into the book, welcome—I'm glad you're here. What you're about to discover—and hopefully cherish—is that this practice is yours alone. There is no *right way* to do anything that follows. I have offered anecdotes and prompts, and even some light direction, but in the end, you are the master of where your pen and paper take you, and the choices you make along the way. Please give yourself permission to adjust the harness, but stay seated with a firm commitment to keep trying.

For me, I usually write non-stop for three pages. Even after 30 years of writing in my journal, some days feel awkward and self-conscious at the start. With persistent effort, and by continuing to show up at the page, my pen eventually accesses a spot that needs some time, attention and intention. What I've often found is that when I get close to the bottom of the third page, I sometimes hit another level of thinking. After moving through the stiff and inflexible top-of-mind ideas—usually my angry or troublesome thoughts—if I stay with it, a fourth page emerges, almost without effort. Have you ever held a yoga stretch for a little longer, and then found another one or two degrees of greater release? Writing can be just like that. Therefore, I encourage you to hold your pen for a longer stretch, especially on days that start off slowly.

Again, this is my process. Yours will follow its own course. That said, if time is one of your most precious and limited commodities, I encourage you to budget 10 minutes for reading and 20 minutes for writing, and see how far you get. You can also do some deep breathing, and feel free to come back to finish a given day's writing at another time.

If you simply cannot find the time to take time, then consider finding a small way to get started—perhaps give yourself the gift of a pad of coloured sticky notes to keep on your desk. Or, maybe you can start a household (or office) gratitude jar that will become a testimony to various moments of joy. You may wish to make lists on a white board or cork board, and transcribe them into your journal once a week. Even when studying bullet points, lines of poetry, or photos on your phone, take time to read each day's background information, and look for reasons to be grateful. After all, gratitudes show up in many ways, and there is no denying that keeping a hand-written record is the best way to track your imagination.

Now is a good time to take the quiz on page 182. Let's begin.

Introduction Notes

[2]   My go-to source for the Precautionary Principle is the International Institute for Sustainable Development, https://www.iisd.org/system/files/2020-10/still-one-earth-precautionary-principle.pdf.

[3]   Antoine de Saint-Exupéry. *The Little Prince*. United States. Harcourt, Brace & World, Inc. 1943. p. 70.

DAY 1:

ENTER WITH A POSITIVE STATE OF MIND

Begin your writing practice with ease, joy,
and a commitment to be kind to yourself.

When my children were younger, they were in various athletic programs. Our eldest and youngest—Philip and Heidi, respectively—skied at the highest level of international competition, as cross-country ski-racers. Our other two, Angela and Matthew, excelled at varsity volleyball, rugby, mountain biking and strength training.

Early in their sporting careers, as parents, we were introduced to the Athlete Development Model (ADM), which put our family on a trajectory of physical literacy, enjoyment of sports, and active mind-body habits that continue to influence our lives.

Other than exercise, my daily writing practice is my prominent life-coping skill. Therefore, I've chosen to revise the ADM acronym to my personal WDM model (swapping in *Writer* for *Athlete*). Through this self-development plan, I have trained myself to write on a regular basis.

When starting any new habit, or trying a training regimen for the first time, it helps to set out with a positive mindset, while silencing your negative biases. As you give yourself permission to experiment and get curious, you can customize your journal practice in the way that makes sense for you. First, you must believe in the importance of the activity.

Like training to be a high-performance athlete, each day will be different. Some days will be better than others, and many will not go as you planned. The goal of training yourself to write—and to find gratitude—begins by growing your awareness. In the early phase of learning, you may need to slow things down as you pay attention to life's sweetness, and fuel your days with greater clarity and efficiency.

Over time, your writing habit can become your personal accountability coach. With practice, you will show up as you want to be seen, track the memories you want to keep, and release those you wish to abandon. Whether your training goals include better psychological, physical, interpersonal or spiritual health, layering gratitude into your writing practice will keep you on track.

What writing style or form will you choose? You may lean toward bullet points, or full sentences embroidered with drawings, sketches, illustrations or photos. Maybe you will write a song or a lyrical poem. The shape of your words is yours to explore—there is no wrong way. The commitment to try and begin with positivity is the first decision.

No matter what you are training for, the challenges you face, or the road you are travelling, a good writing practice will help you find courage, set priorities and frame your living story with a new, life-affirming perspective. Begin with the following:

- A pen (or pencil)
- A journal
- Permission to say whatever you need to say (no filters)
- Comfort (where you're sitting, what you're wearing, what's around you, etc.)

- A plan to read for 10 minutes, write for 15 – 20 minutes, and permission to spend part of this time breathing and thinking when silence rises between words
- The space and privacy you need to attend to yourself and the page (remove distractions, or remove yourself from them)
- A designated spot to securely store your journal when not writing
- Encouragement to experiment as you settle into a style that aligns with your mood and place in the world

Lastly, keep this Chinese proverb in mind: "The faintest ink is better than the best memory." In other words, *thinking* about doing this is a good start; however, by making the time and investing in the effort to write in a journal, you will actually gain the benefits.

YOUR DAY 1 WRITING PROMPTS

1. Read the prompts below, then follow your instincts:

- What prompts have you previously relied on in order to get started, or to keep going? Make a list of things that have helped you jump into writing before.
- Note today's date, and the time of day. Does the calendar or clock hold significance to you right now?
- Rate your energy levels on a scale of 0 (cratering) to 10 (sky high). Where are you in your emotional, social, physical and/or spiritual journey?
- What is energizing you these days? What drains you? How would you describe the spectrum that exists between these two?
- If you like to fill in the blanks, try some of these starts:

- I am so excited about _____
- That said, I am really dreading _____
- I would feel better if I could talk to _____, or hear the following: _____

Here are a few other prompts to consider. Feel free to come back to these at any point in time.

- Name a person or a group of people who have helped you recently. Who are they? What was the nature of their help? What type of energy did they bring to helping you?
- What roadblocks are rising up around you right now? Conversely, what paths are opening for you?
- Share an insight into a small annoyance, or something that's rubbing you the wrong way. Consider starting a sentence, "Something that is really bothering me right now is…" Can this bother lead to a gratitude you may not be aware of?
- Note up to five things that recently made you smile, and label them "My Gratitudes."

2. As you wrap up your writing, put your journal in a safe place. For the rest of the day, and until you write again, commit to paying attention and making mental notes of small moments of joy, and/or reasons to smile, no matter how fleeting.

3. In addition, begin making mental note of the thanks you give to other people. How does giving thanks—expressing gratitude—make you feel? Also, make note of the people you thank, whether you thank them with a silent prayer or out loud. Try to keep track of your thoughts, and write them down the next time you return to the page.

DAY 2:

GET COMFORTABLE BEING BY YOURSELF

Discover what it means to empty your
thoughts into a journal.

I call each writing entry a part of my *Good Morning Pages.* My mom used to greet me each morning with a cheery "Morning, Lorrie," two words she blurred into sounding like *morning glory.* It was a lovely welcome to greet each day. Today, my pages offer me a similarly warm and gentle awakening.

In 1995, I finally committed to the ritual that helps me transition from nighttime dreaming to being fully awake. I had been experimenting with writing in a journal for a few years by then. Ever since the habit took hold, I have been an early riser, choosing to wake in the pre-dawn hours, make myself coffee and shuffle to my desk in my pajamas. Whether at home or on holiday, reeling with anxiety or trembling with delight, a blank page is a treat I still give myself on a daily basis.

For me, writing in the early morning holds a delightful anticipation. What will I learn about myself today? What new ideas will bubble up? What will my journal help me discover? How can I get over the things that are really grinding my gears?

For more than a quarter century, keeping my morning pages has been my single best habit, always helping me find energy, insight and motivation. It may not help me find answers to life's biggest mysteries, but my journal practice helps me unpack swirling questions and challenges on a daily basis. It has become so ingrained as a ritual that when my children were younger, if they noticed I was particularly cranky, they would ask playfully, "Mom, did you skip your writing today?"

While my best time to write is first thing in the morning, it may not be best for you. Perhaps your energy aligns with late night or midday writing. Or, you might decide to split things up—perhaps you will write your pages of responses to whatever in the morning, and make a list of gratitudes before bed. Eventually, you will find your preferred time of day, and the right place that defines your ritual. Whatever you decide, writing can help calm your mind, and give you new ways to enjoy your moments of solitude.

Through the years, people have asked me why I stay with pen and paper, as opposed to using a digital or handheld device. Writing by hand takes time and slows my brain down to the speed of a pen moving across the page. It is a physical process that activates memory, engages the imagination and triggers emotions. When I write in a journal, the past, present and future mix and mingle with ease. In this way, the journal becomes a liminal space, a container of words rooted in my lived experience, and a vessel for transcending the boundaries of time. The process requires no special talent, equipment or power cords, and can literally move me into a dreamscape of possibilities at virtually no expense.

The act of writing by hand narrows my focus to the moment, but also expands the dimensions of time. If I am writing and my ideas feel too elusive, I can reel myself in, centre myself in the moment and keep writing with the words, "Okay, right here, right now, I am thinking..."

No matter what the future holds, in the very moment I am writing, breathing, concentrating and paying attention, I gain a sense of control, and some reassurance that everything will work out well.

Some mornings I am proud of what I write. Other mornings, I leave the page hurriedly, vowing to never look back at those words again. In truth, I seldom re-read what I have written. Rather, I see my journal writing as a reflective process—a type of meditation that clears my head and helps me figure out what I am really thinking. It's a private practice where I can rant, insult others with wild abandon, or celebrate whatever is sitting in my heart. In that way, it's a form of mental hygiene that helps me purge the thoughts that must go away.

As you sit with a pen in your hand, I hope that you can connect the ideas in your head and the emotions in your heart to the blood flowing in your veins. When you do, you can shine a brighter light on all of the good things that might otherwise go unnoticed. Once you get going, you'll discover that your writing practice helps you make sense of your current reality, and establish your priorities. It can also help you process frustrations, unpack lingering puzzles, and set priorities that need action.

YOUR DAY 2 WRITING PROMPTS

1. Ask your head to talk to your pen as if talking to a familiar friend. The most important thing is to start, and assume that you are starting at the beginning...as a beginner. Ask your *pen friend* to write...

    - Today's date
    - Your setting (with as many descriptive details as possible)

2. Now, have your pen friend complete the following sentences:

   - Today, the big thing I am thinking about...
   - I would really like to start by saying…
   - I am feeling…

3. If you feel stuck, ask yourself with delight and self-compassion, "What is going on, and what do I want to accomplish today?" If you are writing at the end of the day, flip the question to ask "What did I accomplish today?" or "What do I really want to accomplish tomorrow?"

4. Close out today's writing by taking six deep breaths. Then, write five things for which you are grateful.

After you set your journal in its safe place, take a few more cleansing breaths, and allow the experience to sink in before you continue with the rest of your day or evening.

DAY 3:

MAKE YOUR NEW HABIT DESIRABLE AND RELEVANT TO YOUR IDENTITY

A good habit sticks when it relates to who you are,
and what matters most.

Writing may be hard for you, especially at the beginning of this journey. Take heart, as it is a challenge to start any new habit. In order to carry it forward, you must believe it is good and worthy of your time. You also must start seeing yourself as someone who writes in a journal.

Earlier, I shared my thoughts on how writing with pen and paper is the best way to start this habit. This old-fashioned approach activates your mind at many levels, including:

- **Physical** – while writing, you are using the muscles in your hands, fingers, shoulders and upper back. Don't forget to breathe deeply and engage your core muscles as you sit.
- **Emotional** – you are writing about your feelings and interior landscape.
- **Social** – you are writing about your personal ecosystem, including the people who are part of your story.
- **Intellectual** – you are using cognitive processes as you consider whatever, putting thoughts into words, remembering recent conversations, anticipating or reflecting on current events.
- **Spiritual** – you are using words to express something that comes from another dimension within you. Whether you want to name it your third eye, source, higher power, or

the universe itself, writing provides a soulful connection to things that lie beyond.

- **Temporal-spatial** – in the present moment, you are writing about your past and/or your future. As you note what's happening around you, you are simultaneously remembering the past and planning for the day to come. When writing, it's my experience that time and space collapse in ways that are similar to what happens in dreams.

In the end, any habit becomes a personal pattern of thought and response that drives action. We hear a piece of news, receive instructions or have a conversation, and we respond in our usual way, most of the time. After a cue or some triggering event—and depending on how we are wired—we may reach for a piece of chocolate, a glass of wine or the cellphone. Habits such as these seldom require much thought, unless there is a disruption or disturbance. The change could be as dramatic as a global pandemic, or as simple as a sudden shift in plans. Either way, our habits can get jiggled and may need to be revived.

Author James Clear advises that when a habit is identity-based, as opposed to outcomes-based, we have a greater chance for sticking with it. He also suggests that habits will have a greater chance of sticking if we bundle our new habits into a package that includes things we enjoy doing.[4]

If you can make some decisions about your identity and how you want to show up in the world, your habits will help you get there. Therefore, as you continue to move forward on this journey, remember to begin as you wish to continue. Decide if you want to be a person who writes in the morning, in the evening, in bullet point form or in flowery prose or poems.

Developing a new writing habit, especially if it feels like homework in the early days, will take some self-talk, gentle encouragement, persistence and patience. As you repeat it, new pathways will start forming. Also, think about stacking or combining your writing habit with something else you enjoy. Will a hot cup of coffee or tea trigger your mind to make the writing connection?

If you choose to put your words down right before bed, that will become your ritual. "I have brushed my teeth, now it's time to write in my journal and get ready for tomorrow." As you train your thoughts to spark actions and patterns of response, you will gain a new and exciting skill.

In my life story, I started a journal practice to help me process events that were confusing and accelerating at a time when my life felt very full. In the early 1990s, my children were young, I had some important personal goals, and my husband was routinely working 12-hour days. The fates of our family's businesses were precarious, and our economic lifelines felt flimsy. I wanted to be part of the solution to various issues we faced, and was motivated to participate in community conversations that occurred outside of the home. I also wanted to juggle the demands of others while keeping my own plates in the air, my marbles in my head, and my essential rocks in the jar of life.

Today, my habit looks something like this: I rise early, make coffee and head to my desk. I don't need to think about checking my cellphone, taking a shower or stretching. For 30 minutes, I enjoy a quiet transition out of sleep. My writing gets me to the starting line of the day to come. My journal is a safe place where I think about issues, and define simple priorities for the day. Within its pages, I dream in technicolour, vent with abandon and talk to myself about everything.

In the living laboratory of family and community, my writing habit helps me unpack many reasons to feel grateful. In so doing, it also helps me:

- Clear my mind.
- Establish my priorities.
- Reframe my issues with greater self-awareness and a fresh perspective.
- Reassess relationships—at home, work and play.
- Be kinder and more understanding. Some days, getting to tolerance is an aspirational goal.
- Remember sad events with greater tenderness.
- Think about losses and things I am missing, even if it is as mundane as a set of keys or an overdue library book.
- Imagine possibilities with optimism and hope.
- Remember to connect with people who inspire me, especially friends and family members who are helpful, kind, fun, energetic, or perhaps hurting in some way.

As for your budding writing habit: perhaps you're finding your way into an evening ritual that helps you leave the day behind. Or, maybe your pages call to you first thing in the morning. Whatever shape your habit is beginning to take, go there in a way that matters to you.

YOUR DAY 3 WRITING PROMPTS

When you have an identity that you wish to express, your habits can help you arrive. And, if you have character strengths that you want to polish and play to, your levels of health and well-being will rise.

The Values in Action (VIA) Institute on Character has identified the following 24 character strengths, organized below according to six defined virtues:[5]

Wisdom Strengths	Courage Strengths	Humanity Strengths	Justice Strengths	Temperance Strengths	Transcendence Strengths
Creativity	Bravery	Love	Teamwork	Forgiveness	Appreciation of Beauty and Excellence
Curiosity	Perseverance	Kindness	Fairness	Humility	Gratitude
Judgement	Honesty	Social Intelligence	Leadership	Prudence	Hope
Love of Learning	Zest			Self-regulation	Humor
Perspective					Spirituality

1. Review the chart of character strengths, and choose four or five strengths that you value and would like to cultivate. Begin your writing with the following: "I would like my writing habit to help me in my wish to identify as _____."

2. Create a *notes to self* section in your journal, as you define a ritual that could make your writing practice more interesting, meaningful and fun. For instance, is there a special spot you could define as your favourite writing space that aligns with your emerging identity? Write a few words about this identity. For example: "I like the idea that I am zesty, keen and energetic because..."

Thinking about this new habit and your identity, fill in the blanks:

- Because I am working on this strength, my favourite writing place(s) should be _____.
- A good ritual for me when writing includes _____. (Does lighting a candle or burning incense sound attractive?) Or, "I would like to bundle my writing habit with_____." (Consider an identity-based routine such as morning meditation, coffee, bedtime tea, etc.)

3. Close with: "I cherish my privilege to…" and keep writing until five gratitudes bubble up.

Day 3 notes

[4] James Clear, *Atomic Habits: An Easy & Proven Way to Build Good Habits and Break Bad Ones*. Random House Business Books, Penguin Random House UK. 2018. pp. 31, 74.

[5] Ryan M. Niemiec & Robert E. McGrath, *The Power of Character Strengths: Appreciate and Ignite Your Positive Personality*. United States, VIA Institute on Character. 2019. pp 26, 27. This classification system stems from a study that surveyed tens of thousands of people living across the globe. In addition to the survey, researchers also reviewed the literature of world religion and philosophy. The list of 24 strengths were identified as "those qualities that are universally considered to be the strongest parts of being human." The list of human traits (as opposed to temporary states) are traits that "other people tend to admire, respect and cherish." When gratitude is developed as a trait, it improves an individual's well-being and sense of purpose, and adds to life's meaning.

DAY 4:

THE SCIENCE OF GRATITUDE (AND ONE OF MY MOST GRATEFUL MOMENTS)

Commit to keep your journal writing practice going— gratitude is in there, somewhere.

Gratitude can motivate you to work harder for the things you value. With improved awareness of yourself and others, trust grows, relationships flourish, and you begin to view yourself with greater self-compassion and mindfulness.

Gratitude has been studied across many disciplines, including psychological, social, physical, metaphysical and spiritual. While gratitude may continue to defy easy definition, it is typically associated with happiness, and is the opposite of resentment. Most importantly, the science behind these feelings is clear: a grateful mindset benefits the body, brain, mind and spirit, and leads to better social connections.

According to Dr. Robert Emmons, a leader in gratitude research, gratitude is a way of seeing the world that can alter our gaze for the better.[6] As Emmons explains, gratitude emerges from a two-step process. First, something happens, and you process the positive, uplifting feelings. Maybe you are enjoying a good cup of coffee, or listening to soothing music. Perhaps you are watching a magical sunset in the company of a good friend, or happily alone. In that moment of gratitude, you stop and affirm to yourself, "Ah, this is so good. I feel grateful." As you pause and appreciate a truly authentic moment of pleasure, the second part of the process begins. You think about where the good feelings came from. Identifying both parts—the initial feeling of awareness, and then locating its source—are key early steps when you're making your way toward gratitude.

Here are some facts about gratitude that my lived experience validates:

- Writing in a journal and making gratitude lists improve my self-awareness and emotional intelligence.
- Tracking gratitudes reduces my levels of fear and anxiety.
- Being grateful helps me get unstuck, gain traction and find motivation.
- Gratitude reduces my cravings for more stuff, and I feel satisfied with what I have.

Here are some facts that Emmons shares from his research:

- Keeping a gratitude journal for 14 days reduced perceived stress and depression in health-care practitioners.
- People who practice gratitude have lower levels of cortisol, the stress hormone, and thus improved heart health.
- People who practice gratitude consume less dietary fat.
- People who were feeling suicidal gained hope and optimism after writing a letter of gratitude.
- People experiencing chronic pain and insomnia show improved sleep quality, and lower levels of depression when they practice gratitude.

In one 10-week study, Emmons separated participants into three groups: the first (gratitude cohort) noted their reasons to be grateful; the second (hassles cohort) tracked their hassles; the third (control group) remained neutral. The study found that participants in the gratitude cohort had fewer health complaints, were more likely to help others, and exercised nearly 90 minutes more per week than those in the hassles cohort.[7]

When we combine this finding with the research that daily exercise is one of the best ways to cope with stress, we start to see a cascading spiral of positivity that links our systems to gratitude. There is conclusive evidence confirming that "exercise may be the most effective instant happiness booster of all activities."[8] Indeed, gratitude may just be the key to enjoying more exercise, new health benefits, better sleep, and a mood swing that shifts away from loneliness, negativity and sadness. You could say that people who stay with gratitude for the long haul are setting themselves up for the many benefits of a natural anti-depressant.

Studies also confirm that there are no known toxic side-effects to a good gratitude practice. By good, I mean gratitude that is expressed authentically, and without any external compulsion. If you can motivate yourself to track gratitude, you will treat your body and brain to flushes of dopamine, serotonin and other happy neuro-transmitters. And, you can track the following within yourself:

- Levels of happiness and well-being
- Levels of perceived stress
- Activity levels and heart health
- Interpersonal relationships at home, work and beyond
- Levels of inflammation in the body
- Levels of hope and optimism
- Thought patterns and default switches that indicate new neural connections in the brain

On a personal note, gratitude has been a centring force in my life for many years. I recognize gratitude as a great rush of relief, and a release of worry or fear. In my numerous moments of profound gratitude, an exuberant exhalation slips from my chest, and I say, "Phew! Thank goodness!"

These days, my world is nourished by many positive relationships. This was not always the case, and I know that life is fragile. Bad things have happened before, and disappointments are familiar to each of us. Our life's circumstances can spin in a negative direction with an unexpected whisper. Staying grounded in gratitude works as a protective coating that nurtures a spirit of resilience, hope, and optimism, and bolsters social connections.

It's easy for me to remember my first life-altering moment of gratitude. In 1983, there were no reasons to suppose that the delivery of our first baby would be anything other than natural and normal, without complications. However, as the moment of birth drew near, I became vaguely aware of a significant shift in the energy of the delivery room. There were urgent whisperings as the doctor leaned close to my ear. He advised me to relax, breathe deeply and resist any urge to push. The baby was in distress, and a surgeon from another hospital had been called.

That was an unexpected challenge. Have you ever been asked to relax in the middle of a moment of climactic intention and urgency? As counter-intuitive as it was, I shifted my mind to thoughts that were very, very small. A nurse calmly coached me to slow my breathing, "In…two, three, four. Out…two, three, four." I registered a quick flicker of relief when the door swung open, and the surgeon walked in. I soon lost consciousness as the anesthetic mask lowered to my mouth.

Hours later, as I held our precious newborn, tears of gratitude, relief and wonder fell down my cheeks. I counted Philip's fingers and toes, and my delight was profound. The following day, the doctor admitted that he was surprised the baby was so lively, and asked if we'd noted the red mark on his neck. That was where the umbilical cord had been wrapped tightly, threatening to strangle him at the moment of birth. My story could have had a much different outcome than the one that settled on the positive side of fantastic brilliance and delight.

As I conjure the memory, I realize it is an inventory of excitement, anticipation and extreme fear, flooded with relief, exhaustion and yes—life-affirming gratitude. It's amazing to think of everything that had to happen in order for the miracle of a healthy newborn baby to be placed in my arms.

Today, I am perpetually excited by the rippling effects that a good gratitude practice can generate, but I know that the path to gratitude is not linear. Keep writing! Stay with the process, wherever it takes you.

YOUR DAY 4 WRITING PROMPTS

At the cusp of our Day 4 writing practice, you may not be feeling gratitude yet. I encourage you to continue to nurture and personalize your practice. Look inside. Look outside. In so doing, you'll develop a strength of character and discipline that can generate greater hope and optimism.

1. What does gratitude mean to you? Can you remember a time when you felt profound relief and a flood of gratitude? How did you feel, and what were you thinking? Did you say anything? Who else was with you? Think about

what had to happen in order for that sweet moment to occur. Describe the scene.

2. Write five gratitudes, using the following structure: "I remember feeling so grateful/joyful/delighted when I was with _____ and we were _____."

Day 4 notes

[6] Robert A. Emmons, *The Little Book of Gratitude: Create a Life of Happiness and Wellbeing by Giving Thanks.* Great Britain: Octopus Publishing Group Ltd. 2016. p. 20 – 21.

[7] Robert A. Emmons, *Thanks! How Practicing Gratitude Can Make You Happier.* United States. Houghton Mifflin Harcourt Publishing Company, 2007. p. 30.

[8] Sonja Lyubomirsky, *The How of Happiness: A New Approach to Getting the Life You Want.* United States. Penguin Books. 2007. p. 245.

DAY 5:

TESTING THE GRATITUDE WATERS IN COMMUNITY

Gratitude is a point of connection, even when
our worlds are wobbling.

When COVID hit, it was as if our entire planet was off-kilter and reeling. As a conditioned community helper, I found myself wondering, "How can I help and support others?" while recognizing that my own bearings were slightly unreliable.

I knew we were all swimming in the same water, more or less, in our *together alone-ness*. Some of us were safe and secure, able to manage solitary spaces with ease. Others were feeling the dark side of isolation and disconnection more acutely.

Having already begun my deeper inquiry into the science of gratitude, I saw gratitude as a path through which others could find new ways to face the challenges of the budding pandemic. Our usual systems of social support were eroding, so I invited some of my contacts to join me for an inaugural five-day online series called *Gratitude Goes Live*. It was a chance to discover how well the gratitude lessons I was learning would resonate with others, and to explore the world of still-new-to-many video conferencing technology.

I asked my first 10 participants to answer some questions. Everyone agreed that they would like to find a practice that could help them accept life as it is, trust the universe's strange new patterns of unfolding, and reduce their individual urges to be in control. Practicing gratitude was my suggestion, and it worked.

I thought that paying attention and listing their reasons to feel grateful would offer a lift, and I was partially right. My error in design was to assume that five days was enough time for people to develop a writing habit that would serve each person equally for tracking gratitudes. I now know that five days is merely the beginning, and something closer to three months is a better timeline when trying to build a habit that sticks. (As an aside: the inaugural five-day workshop soon blossomed into a regular online gratitude gathering, and the most recent sessions have been once a week for eight weeks.)

During that first workshop series, I encouraged participants to slow down, breathe deeply and pay attention to the minutiae of life. Their task was to notice and record things that were going well, while also noting things that were going less well. We started each gratitude conversation with the following ABCs:

- Accept our differences
- Be kind to yourself and others
- Count your blessings

This became the recurring tone for each session, as participants shared what was going well, what could be better, and what they were truly savouring. In the process, our group unearthed and shared stories related to this precipitous moment in time. With COVID-19 keeping us locked in place, we were grateful for birds, sunrises, sunsets, and the connections that our remote meeting space created. Nothing was perfect, of course—we missed hugs, coffee dates, going to the gym, and seeing our kids off to school. Still, each day's conversation focused on moments of joy and delight. One participant even shared her technique for happy dancing alone in the kitchen, with her favourite song blaring loudly.

People confided that our meetings were helping them become more alert and attentive to their surroundings. With better observational skills, they found new reasons to write and define their gratitude lists. Even as COVID-19 had us wobbling, turning our norms into anomalies, we began to see many points of connection. This simple community exercise, rooted in gratitude, was helping us all cope.

Reflecting on the experience more than a year later, it has only strengthened my conviction that gratitude is a powerful social glue, and a solid foundation for building trust. True, gratitude means different things to different people, and convening a conversation themed around gratitude is a potentially tricky exercise. It may take courage, as you risk being vulnerable if you participate fully and authentically within your current trajectory of life. I remain humbled and grateful for the trust those first 10 people placed in our fledgling process.

By intentionally looking for the things that were going well, *Gratitude Goes Live* participants found camaraderie, companionship and comfort, even as we met in the cold waters of a video conference. With subsequent groups and surveys, more than 50 people have provided valuable and validating feedback related to the science of gratitude, from the ground up. In short, gratitude is a motivator and a connector that realigns perspectives. More than anything, I was amazed, delighted and thrilled at the trust we created in our safe, welcoming and supportive listening space. By convening the group with our ABCs, our gratitudes grew stronger.

YOUR DAY 5 WRITING PROMPTS

1. Write your way into the scene, and think about the waters you are swimming in or travelling across. Use your imagination and think about your life and your fellow travellers. Consider your comfort, mood, personal weather patterns, aspirations, and even your limitations. How would you describe the waters you are in? Rough? Smooth? Turbulent? Are things flowing steadily? Is something holding you back? Are you in a life raft, or swimming with water wings? Is your boat stuck in a jam? Moving happily along? How about your provisions? Are you well-stocked? Do you have what you need, including the right bait to catch the big fish?

2. If you'd prefer, switch the metaphor to an environment with which you have a stronger connection. Perhaps you're climbing a mountain, exploring a canyon, birdwatching or looking for shells on the beach. Feel free to make a sketch, or cut a photo from a magazine, and enjoy a moment of playful fun. Give today's session a title and a date.

3. Once you've defined your metaphorical place, make a list of five reasons to be grateful for the gear and/or skills that keep you safe and comfortable (whether boat or boots, fishing line or hammock, etc.). Keep your pen moving as your eyes scan the horizon that your mind's eye creates.

DAY 6:

ABOUT THOSE VOICES IN YOUR HEAD

Writing in your journal increases levels of self-awareness,
self-compassion, and ultimately self-acceptance.

Howard Gardner, an American developmental psychologist, predicts that as the pace of change continues to accelerate, we will need to develop skills that help us stay flexible, resilient and adaptable. To do so, we must cultivate what Gardner refers to as our *five mindsets*, which he defines as follows:[9]

- **Disciplined** – helps us focus on and commit to personal expertise, as we grow toward mastery.
- **Synthesizing** – helps our minds organize massive amounts of information as we seek to understand and communicate with others.
- **Creating** – if we can open our minds to enjoy creative questions, we will find new insights.
- **Respectful** – as we figure out how to work, play and enjoy the company of others, we will better respect and accept our differences.
- **Ethical** – with good rules, and fair, ethical boundaries, we fulfill our obligations as people in relationships with teammates, co-workers and fellow citizens.

I suppose we're all on the spectrum for each one of these mindsets. In fact, my writing practice has helped me realize that I have many minds vying for my time and attention—sometimes all thinking at once, creating a terrible rabble in my head.

One sunny morning, I was sitting at a patio table beside a rooftop pool in Puerto Vallarta, Mexico. I was relaxed, delighted to be on vacation, and writing in a wonderful location that felt very close to heaven. My mind was feeling alive. In that space, I playfully identified and named four distinct voices clamoring in my head at once. These voices were not new arrivals, but on that morning I decided to pay attention to them in a way I had not done before.

The first and most common is the voice of my mother. In fact, I call this voice Dora, after my mother. She is a constant companion and solid reality check—a gentle critic who encourages me to keep trying.

The second voice belongs to my ever-present imaginary friend, Diana. She has been with me since I was six years old. As a relic of my past, she has excellent ideas, and shows up as a capable, courageous and strong girl. When I was a child alone in my bedroom, I talked aloud to Diana, and she was always the winner of any game we played.

The third voice is my inner critic, named Dim-Wit. She is the negative saboteur, always quick to speak up in a spontaneous, highly critical manner. She sounds a bit like an over-protective big sister who goes too far. She knows my flaws, names my insecurities, chastises me and points out my shortcomings—not to protect, but to stifle. She often takes up too much space, and makes quite a racket.

Finally, there's Dobby, who happened to be holding court in my brain on that particular morning. Named after Harry Potter's house elf, my Dobby is a creative, unpredictable, and mischievous voice of distraction. Many of her off-kilter ideas show up on the page, often embarrassing me because they sound so immature and naïve. Still, Dobby says things that intrigue me, since every good house elf sees potential in the mess of chaos and confusion.

Some days, limiting it to four voices would be a blessing, especially when it feels like the crowd is talking at once. As you enter into your Day 6 writing prompt, I encourage you to think about your voices, as well as your various minds, no matter how many you count. When you consider them, also consider their shadows, because when taken to the extreme, every strength or weakness has a flip side.

Let's imagine a pendulum swinging through 180 degrees, and consider the shadowy side of Gardner's five mindsets:

- **Disciplined** – can swing us toward a mindset that is stubborn, rigid, inflexible, judgemental and always seeking control.
- **Synthesizing** – can lead to us heaping more and more information into our thinking. I call it *navigating the grey*, when nothing is black or white, but everything holds a possibility. My synthesizing mind can generate feelings of overwhelm, until I get my bearings and locate some essential truths, or find a solid horizon.
- **Creating** – this mind is constantly questing, much like my Dobby, who is never satisfied because she enjoys the mischief, and can always imagine another intriguing scenario.
- **Respectful** – can lead to compliance, and a reluctance to speak up in the face of a wrong. This is the mind that keeps us quiet, not wanting to hurt someone's feelings.
- **Ethical** – this can be the voice of a rule enforcer or a parent who comes off as too opinionated. This type of thinking may even border on intolerance, as it seeks to uphold the rules at any cost, complying with a system that is tilted.

Many of us have a tendency to exaggerate, ignore truths, or perhaps succumb to various interior dialogues that roar as the pendulum swings. Divergent ideas will collide, and our contradictions can be embarrassing. As thoughts settle, it is often the negative biases that harness us back to centre. Our natural default to the negative is a hard-wired response mechanism that protects us from harm.

Sometimes, something happens, and with no time to think, our brains fire in ways that cause us to freeze, flee or stay and fight. Such responses are evolutionary triggers that have kept us wary and safe for millennia. Meanwhile, our inner voices of calm quietly run in the background. When the cortisol and adrenalin begin to regulate, our muscles relax, and levels of oxytocin, serotonin and dopamine rise.

My Dora voice is certainly a messenger of gratitude—most of the time. She's kin with another voice I call Grace, who defines my *really me* thoughts. Grace asks, "Okay, now, what do I *really* want to do? How do I wish to be seen?" Whether posing questions or offering direction, when Grace speaks up, the other voices go quiet.

YOUR DAY 6 WRITING PROMPTS

1. Have some fun with this prompt. Be as playful, serious, scatterbrained or silly as you want. Name the voices that talk to you as you write. Let them take turns at the microphone (but don't let any particular voice dominate the stage for too long). Who steps up first? Who seems a little shy? Which voice wants to take charge?

2. At the 15-minute mark, ask your *really you* voice (similar to my Grace) to make a list of 5 things for which to be grateful in the moment. Does this voice have a name?

Deeper dive: Have you read a good book lately? In the summer of 2021, I read Thomas King's *Indians on Vacation*. Pick it up, and enjoy how this master storyteller writes about visiting Prague in the company of his motley crew of self-sabotaging voices.

Day 6 notes

9   Howard Gardner. *Five Minds for the Future.* United States. Harvard Business School Press, Centre for Public Leadership. eBook Edition. 2007.

DAY 7:

WHAT WILL MOTIVATE YOU TO TAKE UP YOUR PEN AND OPEN THE JOURNAL TODAY?

Keep writing through pain and adversity.

As I wrote at the start of the book, building a new habit is not easy. It takes practice, but the more you repeat something, the stronger your brain's neural connections grow. Eventually, your mind and body will reorganize around a new, exciting skill—but it won't happen overnight.

In his *Little Book of Gratitude*, Dr. Robert Emmons cites the work of neuroscientist Dr. Rick Hanson, who concludes that the brain takes the shape upon which the mind rests. He writes, "Rest your mind upon worry, sadness, annoyance, and irritability and it will begin to take the shape neurally of anxiety, depression, and anger."[10]

Stop and think about this. If we allow the mind to rest upon worry, sadness, annoyance and irritability, we are wiring our brains to be shaped by anxiety, depression and anger. However, when we nudge our thinking toward thankfulness, we are fertilizing our thoughts to grow into gratitude. Over time, and with good training, "the mind can change the brain in lasting ways," as Emmons points out. Try it for yourself. Rather than allow your hardwired tendencies to switch instantly toward fear, write in a direction that leads to more gratitude and grace.

Here's a story: In June 2017, I was hurrying hard to finalize my paid-for-work phase, wrap up my files, and prepare for life's next chapter. I jokingly told people who asked that I was starting my *rewirement*, avoiding the label *retirement*. Our plan was to leave Banff and go on a two-month vacation to visit family and friends, celebrating milestones and reunions. First, my husband and I would fly to Switzerland, his country of birth, where our daughter was ski-training at the time. Then, I would travel alone to see loved ones in southern Ontario.

The plan took a significant twist when, during a bike ride—a mere four days before my last day of work—my bike's skinny front tire caught in a crack on the road, and threw me wildly to the pavement. My elbow took the full force of the fall, but my head, groin and shoulders landed hard in a sequence of unforgiving bumps and bruises.

After hitching a ride to the hospital, the emergency room doctor looked at the X-ray and said, "Your elbow looks like oatmeal. Luckily," he continued, "the orthopedic surgeon is still in the hospital. If you hurry, he will take you into the operating room right away."

I was relieved that I would be able to receive expert care within hours of my accident. By getting the surgery right away, I quickly rationalized, I would still be able to travel to Europe. I hurried my mind to accept the news as it was being presented, and I was admitted to the operating room without delay.

The moment marked the beginning of what became a four-year dance of my nervous system, vacillating between chronic and persistent pain, counter-balanced with a deep and abiding gratitude.

The day after my surgery, a friend stopped by to see me. She asked how I was doing. The pain was significant, and I found it impossible to get comfortable or enjoy decent sleep. In response to her cheery question, I mumbled, "I am so grateful."

My friend looked confused, so I continued. "I knew a car was approaching from behind," I said. "It could have hit me…but it didn't." A flood of gratitudes followed—I'd been wearing my helmet; a passing motorist picked me up and drove me to the hospital; there was no line waiting at the ER; the orthopedic surgeon generously extended his shift in order to put wires and pins into my smashed elbow joint.

The crash and after-effects brought a full stop to everything I'd planned related to hiking, biking, adventure and outdoor fun. We continued with our travel plans, but the next four years became a series of doctor visits, physiotherapy sessions, massages, and finally another surgery that gave me an unexpected but deeply appreciated new hip joint. As I progressed through this phase of pain and disappointment, gratitude helped me cope.

Practicing gratitude in moments of adversity sounds counter-intuitive. However, it was gratitude that helped me deal with toxic emotions such as frustration and regret, and stave off heavier burdens such as depression and grief. Writing helped me narrow my focus, attend to the present, and find resilience in mind, body and spirit. Yes, there was intense pain and sadness, but there was also the kindness of strangers, the willingness and expertise of wonderful health care professionals, and the support of family and friends—all of which played strongly in my favour.

In maintaining my writing practice as best I could through the swelling and extreme discomfort, I had to disregard the shapes that my letters took on the page. With effort, my journal helped me process the pain with curiosity and intentional positivity as I learned to laugh at my limitations.

Prior to my accident, I had no idea that scientists use the word *rewiring*—the same word I was using in place of *retiring*—in reference to the brain and its neuroplasticity. When Emmons writes that gratitude can improve relationships with yourself and others, and increase levels of hope and optimism, he is talking about rewiring. When we feel grateful, gratitude becomes the very tool that reconfigures the brain. The moment of heart-felt affirmation actually drives a cognitive process that has physical and chemical manifestations. Think of it like a hinge: one flange is located in the heart, while the other flange releases the hormones that flood your heart and head spaces. When you call it gratitude, you are recognizing, naming and opening your mind to a new way of being.

The research abounds. Here is a summary of some of the accepted benefits of a good gratitude practice that I can personally attest to, from separate sources:[11]

- Increased happiness and positive mood
- More satisfaction with life
- Less materialistic
- Improved work-related mental health
- Reduced levels of cortisol, the stress hormone
- Feel less lonesome
- Better physical health, including lower blood pressure
- Less inflammation
- Better quality sleep, less fatigued
- More positive, less fearful mindset
- Stronger family relationships
- Greater sense of hope and optimism

- Connections to people who are cheerful, resilient, caring and outgoing
- More accepting of others—more generous in thought, word and deed

By layering gratitude into daily habits, we recognize that we are part of a much broader picture—a grand, universal ecology, if you will. Even during moments of great pain, gratitude can help us see and appreciate the support we're receiving.

To revisit a point I shared in the Day 4 entry, there are two steps to recognizing gratitude. First, you must process an event and affirm that something good has happened. Second, you must realize that the good is coming from a source beyond yourself and outside your control. By realizing how our lives are enriched by external forces, we can start to see and experience the world differently, realizing that we are supported multilaterally: emotionally, socially, physically, spiritually and intellectually.

YOUR DAY 7 WRITING PROMPTS

1. With gratitude, I know that I am not alone, and that things might be worse. After my accident, gratitude helped me find the motivation to stay positive, and writing helped me cope with my pain. How about you? Today, I'd like you to name the things that bring you to the page, and write about a time when you realized gratitude made you feel a stronger connection to someone or something else—even if it was a time of pain, suffering or loss.

2. When you think about that story or memory, which of your inner voices fires up the engine? What happens if you allow one or two other voices to speak today? If it helps,

consider writing: Dear Dobby, or Dear Universe, or Dear Nobody but me…How about inviting your soft voice of inner grace or joy to speak up?

3. Revisit Day 3's Character Strength chart, and make a quick list of five gratitudes to any of the character strengths you choose. Are any other strengths piquing your interest? Write about those, if you wish.

Day 7 notes

[10] Robert A. Emmons. *The Little Book of Gratitude: Create a Life of Happiness and Wellbeing by Giving Thanks.* Great Britain. Octopus Publishing Group Ltd. 2016. p. 26.

[11] Jeremy Adam Smith, Kira M. Newman, Jason Marsh and Dacher Keltner [editors] *The Gratitude Project: How the Science of Thankfulness Can Rewire Our Brains for Resilience, Optimism, and the Greater Good.* United States. New Harbinger Publications. 2020.

DAY 8:

CHECK IN AND MAKE NOTES TO YOURSELF

Be accountable to yourself. This is your process.

By now, I hope you've begun to recognize the power of gratitude, as well as the benefits of building and maintaining a gratitude-focused writing habit. Earlier, on page 23, I mentioned that we'd be checking in on Day 8. After all, cultivating any new habit takes time, focus and plenty of intentional effort. Now, here we are. Today's prompt is an invitation to track your progress and plan your next steps. Are you ready to keep going?

Writing in a journal, looking for reasons to be grateful, and remembering to pay attention are skills that require practice. Whether you recognize it or not, you are already becoming your own personal trainer and coach. In the Athlete Development Model, which I mentioned back in the Day 1 entry, the progression moves from a *training to train* phase of development, towards a *train to compete* phase.[12] We have to prepare ourselves, and get ready to stay in the race. In order to stay with it, the habit you're building must continue to serve you and fit the circumstances of your life. As you commit to going forward, your personal levels of accountability are instrumental with regards to personal growth and building mastery.

In the days that follow, the going may get tougher; finding time to write may become more difficult; staying committed will require you to calibrate, recalibrate, recommit and hold yourself accountable.

Twenty-five years ago, when I began writing my morning pages, Julia Cameron was my first gentle guide and companion. As she writes:

> "I like to think of the mind as a room. In that room, we keep all of our usual ideas about life, God, what's possible and what's not. The room has a door. That door is ever so slightly ajar, and outside we can see a great deal of dazzling light. Out there in the dazzling light are a lot of new ideas that we consider too far-out for us, and so we keep them out there. The ideas we are comfortable with are in the room with us. The other ideas are out, and we keep them out."[13]

Now, as you commit to continuing your writing and gratitude practice, you will very likely be inviting other ideas into your room. How much light are you willing to let them carry in? Which ideas will you focus on? Which ones will you ignore?

YOUR DAY 8 WRITING PROMPTS

1. Now it is time to complete the Gratitude Accountability List on page 184. Read, review, complete and sign the list.

2. As a bonus prompt, consider the dazzling sounds that could come from a Broadway song, a showtune, lyrics, snippets of poetry, or random thoughts that sometimes run through your mind for no apparent reason—specifically ones that bring you pleasure. Make a list of these earworms or *brain worms* as they arise. Say hello, invite them into your writing room, and give them as much attention as they deserve.

   I've always been a fan of Canadian-born poet and songwriter Leonard Cohen. This string of lyrics from his song "Anthem" is one of my favourite earworms. His poetic voice encourages us to pay attention to the glimmers of light that might be flickering in a dark corner of another room in your story:

"Forget your perfect offering
There is a crack
A crack in everything
That's how the light gets in"[14]

Day 8 notes

[12] Learn more about the Athlete Development Model here: https://sport-forlife.ca/long-term-development/.

[13] Julia Cameron. *The Artist's Way: A Spiritual Path to Higher Creativity.* United States. A Jeremy P. Tarcher/Putnam Book. 1992. p. 51.

[14] Leonard Cohen, "Anthem"; from the album *The Future.* Produced by Rebecca De Mornay & Leonard Cohen; released November 24, 1992.

DAY 9:

GRATITUDE AND EMOTIONAL ECOLOGY

Transformational growth through dislocation—social,
emotional, spiritual and intellectual.

At university, I studied biological sciences. I knew that if I was ever going to learn about how Mother Nature works, I would have to study it as a discipline. Along the way, I also studied French, Spanish and German in order to complete the requirements for my Bachelor of Sciences degree. Nearing graduation, I was uncertain about my career path. When I saw an open call to study abroad, I looked myself in the mirror, talked to a couple of professors and submitted two proposals that would offer me a year away, travel fare and a modest living allowance.

Among my top two choices was the chance to study lake ecology with one of the world's leading limnologists. I had grown up within 30 minutes of Lake Erie, and knew about algal blooms and issues related to sewage and nutrient loading. I was worried about Canada's deteriorating water quality, and thought I would like to be part of the country's emerging interest and prioritization of our tremendous fresh water resources. By the late 1970s, we were connecting the dots between air quality, acid rain, wastewater management and human use. The links between phosphates in detergents and toxic blue-green algal blooms were being validated. We also knew that our global population rise, accompanied with increasing levels of industrial activity, had many effects, some of which stressed our fish populations. Soon, the impact of introduced and invasive species such as zebra mussels would be a topic of concern for our precious Great Lakes.

In September 1978, I flew from Toronto to Helsinki, Finland, on a scholarship to study the rehabilitation of freshwater ecosystems. With my language studies in my back pocket, I assumed that I would be able to quickly learn Finnish. My maiden trip by taxi from the airport to my dormitory as a foreign student was a quick lesson in how wrong I was.

I had lost one of my essential powers as a talker, and could not articulate even simple ideas. Being alone is hard under any circumstances, but here I was in a land as a naïve and misunderstood outsider, unable to express myself, and completely cut off from family and friends. I was also on a fairly tight budget, with a stipend of about $300 a month. Anything beyond basic meals would be out of the question, and keeping in touch by telephone or post would be expensive.

My academic supervisor, a knowledgeable and well-respected expert, had little interest in slowing down his pace of busy academia in order to babysit me. My inadequacies outweighed my competencies, and he decided that we would talk further once I had read and studied the lessons buried in the heavy pile of books he placed on my desk.

For the first few months of my residency, I sat in an airless chamber in the National Water Office headquarters and studied the chemistry of water under the light of a dim desk lamp. The readings my supervisor assigned, written by Europe's leading limnologists, were all in German. It was a slow, lonesome and cumbersome process, and the October days soon turned to December darkness. All around me, grey skies above the harbour of the Baltic Sea blurred the horizon between water and land, while I listlessly held an English-German dictionary in one hand, a pencil in the other.

Recasting my memories from that time through the gentle sieve of distance and perspective, I see that my year in Finland was formative and tremendously influential in my future navigation of choices and relationships—family, social, professional and cultural. For one, the study of a lake's ecosystem is a fascinating exploration of the basin's shape, geology and chemistry, the composition of its sediments, and the various uses of land in its catchment area. Whether a lake borders farmland, a pulp plant, or cottages with birch trees and saunas, the greater watershed possesses a myriad of variables and complexities. It's impossible to study a single aspect of an ecosystem without considering the various elements that influence its ecology.

In fact, every ecosystem—whether a natural, social, emotional or personal ecosystem—is a study of how elements interact, and how energy flows between and among its webs of relationships. Gratitude is as important to your personal/emotional ecosystem as earth, wind, sunlight and oxygen are to the health and vitality of a lake, field or village.

YOUR DAY 9 WRITING PROMPTS

1. Think of a time when you were preparing for something transformative, exciting, important, or meaningful. Consider the setting, your mindset, and the other people in the story. Make two lists that track the following:

   - The positives (those things you really want to remember)
   - The not-so-positives (the hassles or things that didn't quite go as planned)

2. Working with both lists, try to tease out a series of gratitudes for every item you track (whether *positive* or *not-so-positive*). You may be surprised to learn that the things you weren't expecting to find are those that continue to positively impact your personal and emotional ecology. My year as a foreign student was transformative and character-building. Here's my list of gratitudes for that time in Helsinki, Lahti and Lapland:

I am grateful that…

- I was honoured with the gift of an Association of Universities and Colleges of Canada bursary, and a living stipend for a transformative year of learning and growing.
- I met a kind and generous community of international students, and one very special Finnish family.
- I found an inner strength of character that I didn't know I held.
- I witnessed the negative side effects caused by men drinking too much vodka.
- I learned how to cross-country ski on world-class trails.
- I learned that nature is a reassuring go-to place, and a reliable friend when feeling lost and lonely.

DAY 10:

EMODIVERSITY—ACCEPTING THAT LIFE BRINGS BLESSINGS AND CURSES

Monocultures put us at risk. As we feel all the feels, and go where positive energy pulls us, we recognize the benefits of diversity.

No matter the context, diversity creates a buffering effect that provides system resilience. In ecological terms, everything is about relationships and energy transfers. Earth. Wind. Sun. Oxygen. Nutrients. Fungi. Bacteria. Decomposers. Builders.

In our everyday language of life, we talk about things like supply, demand, competing, adapting, thriving and surviving—but growth alone leads only to decline and decay. Generally, the story of how our natural world functions is simplified and framed in the context of winners and losers among desirable and undesirable species. Some species and relationships are labelled *beneficial*, others *harmful*.

When we take time to fully understand how our natural systems operate, we realize that everything is connected. A push or pull on one strand of the system has ripple effects and consequences. The same is true at community, family and emotional levels. And, when it comes to our emotional ecology, I consider gratitude as the driver.

In a study entitled "Emodiversity and the Emotional Ecosystem," published by the American Psychological Association, a team of six scientists explored the emotional and interior landscapes of more than 37,000 participants across different countries using an ecosystem model. Relying on statistical analyses and methodologies developed by terrestrial ecologists, the researchers coined the term *emodiversity* to describe our system of human emotions. Their theory concludes that the more emotions we experience in our daily lives, the more robust our emotional ecosystem becomes—and the better we flourish.[15]

The researchers tracked the following emotions, arranged into *positive* and *negative* categories:

9 Positive Emotions	9 Negative Emotions
✓ Alertness	✓ Anger
✓ Amusement	✓ Anxiety
✓ Awe	✓ Contempt
✓ Contentment	✓ Disgust
✓ Gratitude	✓ Embarrassment
✓ Hope	✓ Fear
✓ Joy	✓ Guilt
✓ Love	✓ Sadness
✓ Pride	✓ Shame

Having a full range of emotions is essential for thriving and coping well. Just as biodiversity can help buffer negative events that occur in one corner of the planet, emodiversity can help keep our range of emotions balanced, and prevent negative ones from dominating the interior landscapes of the human ecosystem. By honouring the full arc of the emotional pendulum, we can have a more robust human experience. Some call it *feeling all of the feels.*

As the study indicates, the greater the range of our emotional swings, the better we can recalibrate to changing conditions. If we are angry, for instance, it may be beneficial to our long-term survival to sit with and nurture our anger for a bit before returning to a more neutral place of contentment, or even swing toward amusement rather than lash out in rage. We know that it is not healthy to stay perpetually on high alert, or to live a life under constant stress or fake happiness. Every mother of a competing athlete knows that post-race is not the perfect moment for conversation. The hyper-charged racers need time for their cortisol and adrenalin levels to settle, perhaps even taking a few cool-down laps so their pulses, respiratory, digestive and other internal systems can normalize.

It isn't realistic to try to maintain an emotional state that is 100% of any one thing all of the time. We will be cheery; we will be gloomy. The swing is both natural and healthy. As our most honest and authentic selves, we must become comfortable with the concept of diversity in all of our ecosystems—emotional, social, internal and external.

YOUR DAY 10 WRITING PROMPTS

1. Make a chart with two columns. Label one column Blessings, the other Curses. Then, fill in your chart by writing five blessings, and five curses.

2. Now, borrowing from a writing prompt that I received a few years ago, I'd like you to mash the lists together into a single piece of writing. Have fun as you write a brain dump, song, poem, letter or some nonsensical list of no great consequence. Your goal is to arrive at a place that feels good in its richness and emodiversity (and hopefully an exercise that turns up the corners of your mouth).

Day 10 notes

[15] Jordi Quoidbach, June Gruber, Moïra Mikolajczak, Alexsandr Kogan, Ilios Kotsou, and Michael I. Norton. "Emodiversity and the Emotional Ecosystem." *Journal of Experimental Psychology*. 2014. Vol 143, No. 6., pp. 2057 – 2066.

DAY 11:

WATCHING NATURE, A SOURCE OF WONDER AND AWE

Tap into wonder, gratitude and hope—strengths that connect you to the larger universe and its mysteries.

In your Day 3 writing prompt, we talked about identity, and how you want to show up in the world. As mentioned, when a habit is identity-based, it has a greater chance of sticking. On page 38, I introduced the VIA Classification system of 24 character strengths, and encouraged you to consider the qualities that the scientists behind the study referred to as "universally considered to be the strongest parts of being human."[16] (It may help to bookmark the VIA list as we continue with today's entry.)

It is well known that our natural bias tilts us toward the negative. By focusing on our personal strengths, we can hit reset. Clearly, negative experiences can be formative, and every cautionary tale helps us learn and grow. However, defining ourselves exclusively by our mistakes and losses will only leave us feeling sad and weary. A shift in focus to caring about our character strengths can help us fill in some of the gaps in our self-awareness. Gratitude is one way by which we can expand our narrow narrative, and look toward new horizons.

On the VIA list, gratitude is one of five strengths organized under the *Transcendence Strengths* column. According to the experts behind the study, transcendent strengths relate to accepting that we may never know or fully understand certain things. These strengths are about recognizing that our knowledge is limited, and putting this recognition to good use.

In addition to gratitude, the other four character strengths that align with transcendence, and the mysteries we may never understand, include the following:

- Appreciation of beauty and excellence
- Hope
- Humour
- Spirituality

These strengths tend to exist beyond our intellect. They bring us closer to deep joy, the magical, the unknown and the unknowable. Moments of transcendence are often punctuated with laughter, tears and awe.

My moments of personal transcendence often occur when I'm walking, hiking, skiing or sitting in nature. Many authentically grateful people I know also find inspiration in nature. They form a community of bird watchers, walkers, skiers and hikers who enjoy opening their eyes, ears, noses, hearts and minds widely. Many times, I have heard people equate moments on mountain tops, or walking in a cathedral grove of tall hemlock trees as their version of going to church.

Doing just about anything in nature can reduce stress, help you open your eyes to miracles that surround, and put you back on solid ground. There's a certain slowness to being outside, and navigating a natural landscape that encourages, or even demands that you slow down, pay attention and stay patient. In nature, our senses must adjust to new channels of light, sound, smells and intuitive feelings. We luxuriate or linger at our peril if we miss a foreboding shift in the wind, or remain oblivious to a crack of distant rocks.

I affirmed my love of nature watching in 1993, in the sanctuary of an old-growth rain forest on the Islands of Haida Gwaii, an archipelago of magical proportions off the Pacific coast of British Columbia. The links between the human, natural and spiritual worlds are integral to the folklore and legends whispered in that transcendent space. The islands are home to the Haida Nation, and for five seasons, I volunteered for a research project, studying the impact of introduced species on songbird populations. The collaboration between researchers from France and Canada was a partnership that grew into a 30-year story of research and appreciation of the ecosystem's elements—its ecology, beauty, culture, legends and mystery.

The years of field studies revealed many intricate relationships, intended and otherwise, between humans (locals and visitors), mammals of the land and sea, birds, insects and flora. Across the dimensions of soil, air, sea and seasons, we were privileged to witness the flow of life and processes, evolving along a continuum of change over time.

For several small moments, I sat quietly, observing subtle movements in the dense, temperate rain forest. My official job was to look for birds and determine if a nest was nearby. I would wait patiently and quietly for a bird to flit into view so I could note its behaviour. From my own perch in an ethereal lichen-laced, moss-covered world, I occasionally tried sketching what was around me. In those moments of natural solitude—surrounded by life, yet entirely alone in my human experience—all of my senses sharpened. I felt a tremendous lightness, and was alive in a new way.

When a pair of birds arrived, I would watch their behaviour, listen to their chatter, and decide if they were feeding, courting, fetching materials for a nest or tending to nestlings. If the pair seemed to be busy with a nest-in-the-making ritual, I would describe the site with as much detail as possible, thereby enabling the next observer to continue watching the process. Eventually, the merest flick of a bird's tail would lead me to the thrill of finding a well-hidden nest in a spruce thicket. Later, back at camp and with pen in hand, I would make notes of the day, wiring details into my brain, quieting the chatter of inner voices and distilling tiny details into a rich experience.

Almost 30 years later, my memories from this time are full of wonder and tenderness. I will never forget the feeling of privilege and gratitude as I sat in that landscape, an oasis of ageless beauty and oxygen-rich air. Called the Misty Isles, the soundscape of the forest was silenced at the shoreline, as the ocean waters crashed against rocks with a constancy and thunder. The interplay of sea and shore, and the patterns and mosaics of greens and greys, ferns, fronds and giant banana slugs were beautiful, humbling, awe-inspiring and transcendent. The mysteries revealed in the quiet of those days far exceeded lessons that years in a laboratory or a library could ever unveil.

YOUR DAY 11 WRITING PROMPTS

1. In nature, we find rich and chilling emotions that are personal, precious, transcendent and universal. A chest-thumping hike can kindle a spiritual authenticity you cannot fake. What are a few transcendent or magical wonders in your life? Whether crickets or crows, fireflies or a startling sunset, describe them. Where does your transcendent strength lie? If your spirituality is faith-based and comfortable, use that lens for considering transcendence (defined as follows: *knowing there are things that we can never know or fully understand*).

2. Write down a list of gratitudes you associate with such moments. From there, try your hand at sketching a web diagram. In the centre of the hub, name something transcendent for which you are grateful. Expand the spokes of the hub, noting the forces, energies, people or things that conspired for it to land on your page today. How would you describe this ecology?

Deeper dive: if you are curious about character strengths and virtues, take the VIA test of Character Strengths found at: https://www.viacharacter.org/survey/account/register

You can set up a free account. When you have finished taking the test, make special note of your scores for the following (we'll come back to these later):

Gratitude ____   Love of Learning ____   Hope____
Prudence ____   Judgement____   Self-regulation ____

Day 11 notes

16   Ryan M. Niemiec & Robert E. McGrath [eds]. *The Power of Character Strengths: Appreciate and Ignite Your Positive Personality.* VIA Institute on Character. 2019. p. 221.

DAY 12:

KINDNESS AS A REVOLUTIONARY FORCE, PART 1

Kindness is a character strength, not a human weakness.

Staying with the VIA chart of 24 character strengths, it is interesting to note that Kindness is one of the character strengths associated with *Humanity Strengths*. The other character strengths attributed to humanity include Love and Social Intelligence. These strengths help us in our one-on-one relationships. Long before I began an intentional study of gratitude, I used kindness as a simple navigational guide for endeavours at home, heart and beyond.

It's been said that the personal relevance and meaning behind every idea is connected to the socio-economic-historical and cultural context from which it emerges. In the mid 1990s, as I experienced a number of watersheds, I was definitely in my *quest-for-meaning-and-purpose* phase of life.

A decade and a half earlier, after finishing my studies in limnological sciences, I had moved to Banff, choosing romance over education, parking my dreams related to advanced education and career. By the time I looked up and saw it was the mid-1990s, I was rocking in a phase of transition and flux. We were a family of six by then, a cultural mix of Swiss and Canadian heritages, living in a small mountain town inside of a national park. My husband, Erwin, was our trusted business leader and qualified restaurateur, the hard-working captain of the family's financial ship. At home, our four children were teaching me how to be as kind, caring and patient as humanly possible, lacing my world with the strings of more responsibilities than I had ever imagined.

By March 1995, our main restaurant was forced to relocate to a more affordable location outside of the bustling downtown core, while our second restaurant sank. As our financial watermarks fluctuated, Erwin kept steering from his captain's chair, and I stayed committed to our family and community. I also felt a compulsion to invest my time and energy beyond the kitchen in an effort to better understand our local landscape and factors that influenced the climate of local change and development.

Allow me to back up a moment. A few years before this, the UN's World Commission for Environment and Development released the Brundtland Report, entitled *Our Common Future*, named after former Norwegian Prime Minister, Gro Harlem Brundtland. As a caring citizen with strong environmental values, I assumed that global leaders would embrace the visionary findings, invest in policies to address emerging inequities, and ensure a more sustainable world. In fact, I was certain that the intelligentsia of the world would help us move ahead through a lens of common understanding and shared values. This report introduced the concept of sustainability, and I believed that world leaders would create new systems that valued the environment, economy and social well-being of everyone. Naïve as it may sound, those were my first and most authentic thoughts.

Sadly, I soon realized that the rest of the world did not share my optimistic and confident views. True, daily news feeds discussed issues of environmental and economic sustainability. However, deeper, more intricate matters related to growing populations, politics, the environment and the economy did not receive the specific attention they demanded. Instead, these critical issues were mixed into a stew and served up with divergent ideologies, technological approaches, and cultural practicalities. The result was a dish of disagreements that became a giant, goopy mess.

Zipping back to 1995, I decided I wanted to do something. I chose to volunteer for a federally mandated public participation process, called the Banff-Bow Valley Study. Once a month, I sat at a roundtable of experts who discussed wide-ranging topics related to science, nature conservation, economic development, tourism, regional culture, legal jurisdiction and critical habitat. It was there that I learned about the Precautionary Principle, which I mentioned in the book's introduction. Over the course of 18 months, I bore witness to a process designed to build trust and allow people to share their honest, passionate and often divergent perspectives. I saw how easy it was for people to push the *anger* and *frustration* buttons, while my dear friends *kindness* and *understanding* sat quietly in the corner, watching motes of dust settle in the spit.

I stayed committed to managing our children and household, becoming hyper-alert to the benefits of diversifying our income. More than anything, I wanted to contribute meaningfully to the world, and help support our growing family. In that our children were all now in school, I felt like the moment was here, and my morning journal practice helped me process the pieces of my ever-shifting jigsaw puzzle of life.

On a winter evening in 1996, I was sitting in the gallery of our local museum, listening to June Callwood, a Canadian icon, feminist and social justice advocate. Ms. Callwood was speaking as part of a series that I had helped to coordinate, which explored the theme of "What is Canadian culture?" I sat in the audience as a rapt note-taker, prepared to write an article for a local newspaper which ran under the title: "Kindness defines Canadians: Callwood."[17]

Yes, Canadians embrace an idea of kindness as part of our cultural identity. Ms. Callwood was the first public figure to echo my mother's simple wisdom, saying "kindness is key." For her part, Callwood modeled a type of kindness that was linked to virtues of humanity and compassion—one that demanded that we see people as human beings, putting babies and children as our highest priorities.

My experiences during this turbulent phase of early motherhood and growing into life helped me understand that there are different and sometimes widely divergent world views. Ms. Callwood was generous in her expanded understanding of Canada's cultural and socio-economic structures. She called out the policies that enabled some people to succeed while others were seriously hamstrung by unjust systems of care.[18] Her writing career, professional journalistic approach, feminism, charm, simplicity and deep humanity made her a giant influence on my life. More than anything, her conviction that Canadians hang on to their kindness as a badge of honour still continues to ripple in my mind.

To be continued on Day 13. Until then…

YOUR DAY 12 WRITING PROMPTS

1. When you hear the word *kindness*, what does it mean to you? Have you ever thought of kindness as an antidote to your problems? Is there a name, face or moment from your life (or multiple names/faces/moments) with which you equate kindness? Spend time writing them out, and

thinking about kindness as a strength that can help you in one-on-one relationships.

2. Remember the voices you named on Day 6? Which of those voices speaks loudest when you think about kindness? Or, is there another voice that you associate with kindness? What happens if you allow this voice to guide your writing today?

3. Before you wrap up, make a list of at least five reasons you are grateful for some form of kindness you have received. As you move away from the page, try to remember the person or people who helped bring kindness your way. How did you acknowledge the kindness? In thought? Word? Deed?

Day 12 notes

[17] Widmer-Carson, Lorraine. "Kindness Defines Canadians: Callwood". Canada. Article in *The Banff Crag and Canyon*. February 21, 1996. p. 25.

[18] In 1968, Callwood went to jail for trying to stop police from taking homeless youth, people who were impoverished, adrift and without access to medical care or social supports, into custody in Toronto. (See: http://www.caseyhouse.com/wp-content/uploads/2013/02/JuneCallwoodExtendedBio.pdf.) Her final public interview on CBC television with George Stroumboulopoulos, and a testament to how a courageous woman faces death on her own terms, can be found here: https://www.cbc.ca/player/play/1750347753.

DAY 13:

KINDNESS AS A REVOLUTIONARY FORCE, PART 2

*Kindness is not about patronage or power.
Kindness creates possibilities and connects us as
human beings. Kindness is humble.*

Let's stay with kindness for one more day. Here's a snippet from my morning pages, dated Friday, February 14, 1996 (the morning after I saw June Callwood speak):

> *June Callwood mentioned that she thought Canadian culture was more of an attitude. Kindness, she said is an attitude of caring for one another as well as a kind of anti-revolution. She thinks that Canadian culture is under assault because our politicians are telling us that we can no longer afford to care for one another. Really, I ask? Is it true that we can no longer afford kindness?*

For June Callwood, kindness was a form of social justice that moved her to action. I was inspired by the simplicity of the idea, and admired her dogged advocacy to eliminate childhood poverty and support young people who, as she saw it, had never been given a chance. Around the time I saw Callwood speak, I began looking for meaningful employment that would put me back into the workforce, while keeping our family structure intact. By the mid-2000s, after a decade of contracts and freelancing, I gladly accepted a position as the first paid staff person at the newly formed Banff Community Foundation.

When I started, I wondered what it would take to do my best work for a start-up organization with a tiny budget. I was committed to the sector, felt aligned with community values, and was certain of this young organization's potential. Still, my understanding of the words *charitable* and *philanthropic sector* was half-baked. I had much to learn.

My first lessons related to setting policy, working with a volunteer board of directors, and learning the sector's essential legal framework. For example, we were obliged to act in accordance with the rules of charitable law, the Income Tax Act. We needed accounting systems that allowed us to accept donations, make grants and increase levels of trust in order to grow a community endowment fund—an invested savings account that would serve future generations in perpetuity.

Our signature programs involved making grants to other organizations, but growing the endowment fund required patience and a longer timeline. In accordance with Canadian charitable law, our public foundation needed to serve in one of three ways: for the relief of poverty; the advancement of education; and/or other purposes beneficial to society. The organizational papers decreed that we would not award grants for *direct religious activities*, giving us a mandate to approach our change-inspiring work from the secular side of kindness.

With our focus defined geographically, our community grants program inspired organizations to make innovative proposals that helped people, with a focus on their well-being, in areas of health, education, heritage, arts, recreation, culture and social supports. My job was to attract donations, inspire trust and steward dollars that either paid the bills, awarded grants, or landed in the endowment. All gifts would help the community flourish, given enough time, but some days we wondered how to pay for the electricity.

As the first and only paid staff person in a new-to-community organization, the work felt lonely, and the burden of responsibility was significant. The support structures—including human and financial capital—were fragile. My morning journal ritual was essential for grounding my ideas, and avoiding the urge to grind my teeth or give up.

Happily, and with time, the organization grew into a position of relevance and significance. Before I left my job, the number I was proudest of was the $1 million worth of grants that we had attracted and reinvested as community grants, enabling the work of other organizations.

Organizing community kindness from a 300-square-foot office, with no discretionary dollars for purchasing paperclips, was a challenge that required creativity, imagination and extraordinary grit. With hearts on our sleeves, and the best of intentions, we introduced our community to a culture of philanthropy that was about grant-making and relationships. We launched one of our signature events, called Random Acts of Kindness Day, which we soon began calling RAK. With flour, chocolate, oatmeal, butter, eggs, and a precious family recipe, I baked an extra-large batch of cookies at home. At the office, volunteers wrapped the goodies as gifts and took them to the street, offering cookies to anyone who was brave enough to look us in the eye or say hello. In our own little way, it was a radical act of kindness—giving without any expectation of financial return. The kindness that the cookie-givers delivered was rewarded not financially, but with what is known as *helper's high*. Years later, I read about research that statistically confirmed how "kindness can jump-start a cascade of positive social consequences."[19]

Helping others satisfies a basic human need to connect, win a smile and feel valued. Our volunteers reported happy feelings, and their cheeks were flushed with excitement as they told their stories. Kindness can increase a person's sense of self-worth and heighten an awareness of how it feels to connect with others *in kindness*, especially when they feel appreciated for their effort. People who received the cookies were both surprised and appreciative, and our *RAK-attacks* became part of our organizational story.

Over the years, kindness cookies became symbolic of our efforts to encourage social connectivity, and increase our community's social capital. Our endeavours reaffirmed something I was coming to understand about kindness: the bridges and bonds we form with people grow when we interact positively with one another.

When people act with kindness, whether random or intentional, and when others receive gifts as intended—enjoying the spirit of generosity and benevolence—our levels of happiness and connectivity rise. In that way, kindness can create ripple effects across any town, province or village.

By deliberately cultivating a culture of generosity and kindness, our organization was anchoring our work in the realm of *humanity*—the domain that is strengthened by love, kindness and social intelligence. In organizing ourselves around kindness, with intentional celebrations of micro-generosity, we were also expanding our community's social capital based on our most powerful currency: concern for the benefit of others.

At the end of Ms. Callwood's talk in 1996, she lowered her voice and said, "I see that during these times, our culture is being threatened. We are being told by our politicians that it is wrong for us to care for one another…that we can no longer afford to be kind. The current climate is leading us to believe that kindness is wrong."

The idea that kindness is too expensive, wrong, or a luxury we cannot afford has never sat well with me. I see power in kindness, and the gratitude that grows from acts of inclusion is the social glue that binds hearts, heads and hands to our global village.

The only kindness we cannot afford is one that patronizes, disables or disempowers people, especially those labelled inferior or undeserving of a chance. The kindness we need is human-centric, empowering, encouraging, and elevating—a kindness that lifts people up, and helps everyone feel valued, connected and supported.

YOUR DAY 13 WRITING PROMPTS

1. Using a lens of kindness and gratitude, we can unpack some amazing sequences of events. Today, I encourage you to use a lens of kindness to reframe an event in your life's story. Can you think of a time when you received kindness out of nowhere? Have you ever delivered a kindness that was also an act of defiance in the face of some injustice, or a desire to create change? If kindness is a ladder, where are you standing? Who is standing one rung higher? Who is a few rungs lower?

2. Complete this sentence with five phrases: "I know I am lucky because…" How does looking through the lens of kindness help you complete it?

3. June Callwood left a lasting legacy of what it means to be a kind human *bean*. When she visited Yorkville in the 1960s, she saw and gave her time to young people who were lost, abandoned, drug addicted and looking for home. In the 1980s, she offered warm meals and helped build a home for people stigmatized with a diagnosis of AIDS. Throughout her life, she advocated for frightened young mothers who needed warmth and shelter. One of her great legacy quotes is, "If any of you happens to see an injustice, you are no longer a spectator, you are a participant. You have an obligation to do something." Before you leave the page today, write about the idea of kindness being a revolutionary act.

Day 13 notes

19   Sonja Lyubomirsky. *The How of Happiness: A New Approach to Getting the Life You Want.* United States. Penguin Group. 2007. p. 130.

DAY 14:

MANAGING MEMORIES

Finding gratitude means remembering, reflecting
and seeking fresh insight.

Perhaps it won't surprise you to hear me say that memory possesses its own ecology. Your past is a file folder of life events, and some portals may have been sealed tight, shrouded in mystery and possibly misery.

Feeling grateful is a memory jog, because something had to have happened. First, there was an event that you remember. Then, through the mists of time, you look back and think, "That was good. Actually, that was really wonderful." In hindsight, your deeper levels of the mind might confirm, "Yes, that was lovely." And you continue to muse, "I wonder where that goodness came from?" Sometimes, it can take years before some of us decide to unpack a memory and acknowledge the goodness found within.

Some thoughts trickle back slowly, and often, good deeds are easy to ignore, especially if they were commonplace and familiar. We might get used to good things happening, become accustomed to them and assume that our good fortune is normal for all and forever. Over time, the buzz of any good thing can erode and become the expected norm. Interestingly enough, one person's expectation of standard goodness is another person's aspirational goal.

When we see kindness and gratitude as character strengths, and parts of our identities, we can more readily revisit the past from different points of view. Sometimes, past events hold a type of psychological tension, especially when certain things were left unsaid, or feelings remain unresolved. Sadness and regret may float wordlessly in the midst of a memory.

Dr. Robert Emmons describes past events that were emotionally charged, unpleasant or haunting as being "open memories."[20] It could be a romantic rejection, the loss of a job or an academic failure. Perhaps the memory involves betrayal, theft, a sexual transgression, emotional abuse, physical violence or death.

In addition to realizing that we have open memories, when past events remain unresolved, positive psychology guru Dr. Martin Seligman reminds us that our memories are actually "quite shoddy."[21] After all, if you sit two people in the same room and ask them what just happened, it's unlikely that their stories will match. Parents, lawyers and teachers know this well. We misremember details, make assumptions, get distracted or pay less-than-full attention. Our cognitive thought processes—and the voices in our head—can blur the details.

Memories hold elements of reality, experience, imprecise perspective and cultural bias. When it comes to retelling a story or reporting an event, we tend to remember a mashup of what *actually* happened, and what we *imagine* having happened. What's more, every player and voice in our head takes part in the retelling, and our mind's cast of characters make assumptions that may or may not be true.

Studies demonstrate that when people write in a journal and reframe the open memory with grateful intentions, they find new insight.[22] Recasting the past through the lens of gratitude can help us see things we missed the first time. The point of revisiting an unhappy memory is not to keep reliving or ruminating on sadness, but to reach new levels of insight and awareness.

With my journal as my steady companion, I have returned to many events that occurred during painful periods—often blathering on for many pages. I have spent excessive time and energy, and wandered many hours through the murky shadows of half-remembered experiences in order to land on something with certainty. Sadly, doing so is not energizing, but depleting to the point of exhaustion. Still, it is important to sit with sadness until a tiny glimmer of light shines through, and you can nudge yourself forward.

What's changed over time is that now, instead of entering every room with a sense of indignance or anger, I try to wade through my negative emotions and look for a hidden light switch. Entering the memory chamber through a door of open-minded curiosity can shift the narrative from "This is what I remember," to "I wonder what else was going on?"

According to Emmons, the two primary obstacles to feeling grateful align with what I mentioned above: first, we are forgetful (those shoddy memories again); and secondly, we may have been distracted, or only paying partial attention in any given moment. Yes, forgetting is part of the human condition, and that includes forgetting to feel grateful. When we don't consider the perspective of other people with whom we share a story, or if we only focus on our own little pity-party, we risk being blind to everything else that was taking place.

A word of caution: dealing with the past is not easy, and not every open memory is ready for exploration. These days, I still hear myself asking, "What is the thing that I am trying to forget?" If I remember it, I can say, "That's right, I don't ever want to think about it again." Doing so helps me disconnect the wiring that makes certain memories undesirable, and strengthen the wires to those memories I seek to savour.

Talking about memories with your fellow travellers—those who were there with you, and/or those who knew you then— can be a fascinating and insightful way to revisit certain pain points. There is also the chance that doing so may create more sadness or frustration, but it's your story, and you are the captain of your ship. What watery perspective will you jump into as you write an open memory into a new horizon?

Gratitude is a complex social emotion. As we've explored, it is a strength, skill, attitude and perspective that can pave new paths to the past, especially as we seek to move beyond regret. Processing painful memories is difficult work, and may require professional support. You need to keep yourself safe. It might help to do some pre-work as you narrate and write the story that lives in the personal, private spaces inside your head.

YOUR DAY 14 WRITING PROMPTS

1. Your gratitude-self can open new doors in your memory vault, and close others. Do you have an open memory? Have you ever tried to approach it through curiosity? Assuming you are on solid ground, try recasting the memory, not to relive it, but to understand, "Who else was in the story? What else was going on? What did I forget?" It is possible that certain events from your past actually contain glimmers of light you've been overlooking.

2. Dr. Martin Seligman suggests that if we do not fully appreciate and savour the good events in our past, we may over-emphasize the bad ones. By extension, we may even

invite those culprits who undermine our serenity and life satisfaction to linger longer than necessary. "Gratitude amplifies the savouring and appreciation of the good events gone by," he shares, "and rewriting history by forgiveness loosens the power of the bad events to embitter (and actually can transform bad memories into good ones)."[23]

3. I invite you to make a list of things you know went well in the memories you just touched upon. Then, start a list of dates and places that you'd rather forget. (Note that on Day 26, you will be invited to recast and reframe one of these memories in a curious and grateful way.)

4. Rather than accept that you don't want to remember certain moments, allow yourself a courageous revisitation, and start considering the things that actually went well. Note the sparks of positive energy, hope or opportunities that arose. Look for teachable moments that helped you become the person you are now.

Day 14 notes

[20] Robert Emmons. *Gratitude Works! A 21-Day Program for Creating Emotional Prosperity*. United States. Jossey-Bass. 2013. pp. 140 – 147.

[21] Martin Seligman. "Positive Psychology: Martin E.P. Seligman's Visionary Science." An online non-credit course authorized by University of Pennsylvania and offered through Coursera. Summer 2020.

[22] Simon Makin. "What Happens in the Brain When We Misremember." *Scientific American*. September 9, 2016. https://www.scientificamerican.com/article/what-happens-in-the-brain-when-we-misremember/.

[23] Martin E.P. Seligman, *Authentic Happiness: Using New Positive Psychology to Realize Your Potential for Lasting Fulfillment*. United States. The Free Press, a division of Simon and Schuster, Inc. 2002. p. 70.

DAY 15:

GRIEF SITS RIGHT BESIDE GRATITUDE

There is a quiet to gratitude, as it moves us from grief
in the direction of beauty and transcendence.

Around the same time that June Callwood was influencing me to commit to the power of kindness, my mother, my own benchmark of kindness and love, was losing her independence due to blindness. She was also navigating the implications related to my father's loss of health. His heart and lungs were seriously diseased, and he was tethered to an oxygen tank at all times.

I called home one afternoon from a rocky outcrop of Reef Island. This was my third trip to the archipelago of Haida Gwaii, and our son Matthew was with me. I heard the wispiness of my father's voice when he answered the phone—it was hard to recognize him.

I knew I needed to get back to see both of my parents, and did so as quickly as I could. The moment I set my suitcase down, my sister and I jumped in her car to head to Dad's hospital room. A friend of his was sitting in a chair near our father's bed, looking bereft and crinkled. His upper lip was quivering. "Your father didn't eat any of his dinner," he said.

Dad's eyes fluttered open. He looked at us. "Happy to see you," he said, and gently squeezed my hand. We asked him what he wanted to eat, then ventured out to bring him his favourite drink, a Brandy Alexander—a blend of milk, eggs, honey and brandy, with ice cream and nutmeg on top.

Our father sipped the drink gratefully, and licked the milky froth from his upper lip with joy. His hazel eyes were clear, his face had fewer wrinkles than earlier. In that moment, he seemed to be letting go of worries.

I slept in my old bed that night. The next morning, my mother took me on a garden walkabout. She was delighted that she had been able to find petunias and impatiens with colours that mixed well with Sweet William and juniper. She greeted, touched and smelled the leaves of the foxglove, wisteria and peonies. It was like she was pulling energy out of the plants, gathering her strength, preparing for the day to come.

After her methodical inventory and generous expressions of thanks for her garden, we returned to the kitchen. The phone rang as we were sitting down to breakfast. The nurse on the other end told my mother that Dad had had a bad night. This morning, he was cyanotic—effectively turning blue because of a loss of oxygen in his blood. His condition was now critical.

Back in his room that morning, his small transistor radio was tuned to a local station. The music was cheery, and a breeze danced lightly with the curtains at the open window. Dad was neither alert nor responsive, his breathing was irregular and shallow, and he didn't rouse beyond flickering his eyelids when others came in. We talked softly, chuckling at the idea that his Brandy Alexander may have been his last meal. We watched as his eyelids flicked open, then his chest rose high and collapsed with a shuddering breath.

"That's it," I said. "He's gone."

"Are you sure?" my mother asked. "I have seen him like this before."

I almost started to laugh, knowing that being nearly blind, she was hardly the ideal eyewitness. But I sat quietly, honouring the moment.

"This time he really is gone," I said.

Through sobs, I watched my mother stand up, straighten her dress, put her hand into his and ask that he take her with him. She waited. When no response came, she said in a strong, clear voice, "Jim Carson, it has been an honour and a privilege."

The lumps in our throats kept us speechless after that. My mother had always been the centrifugal force of human kindness in our family. She held our heartstrings, mended shirts and kept the home fires burning at all times. Today, when I reread my journal notes from that period, I realize that in her most profound moment of grief, facing a loss that would unwind her independence and purpose, she had embraced gratitude.

For his part, my father had been the classical patriarch: protector, power-house, bread winner and supreme commander. I can't pretend that I was always happy with his ways of thinking or being in the world, but on every page, and in every chapter and memory, there are reasons to be grateful.

At the reception following his funeral, a friend and bridge partner of his told me of how my father had supported him when his son died. "He was such a comfort," the friend confided. "He knocked on our kitchen door. It was early morning, and I was still in pajamas. He was the first person to come by the house after hearing our sad news."

As the friend continued his story, he used my father's own words from that time to comfort me now.

"We had a coffee and talked for a bit. As he was leaving, your dad put his hand on my shoulder and said, 'You can't do anything about the past. But one day, you might be able to do something about the future.'"

My father's words continue to comfort me long after his passing. Coupled with my mother's powerful declaration in the moment of his death, I am convinced that gratitude passes through grief, moves through beauty, and helps us catch a glimpse of shimmering transcendence.

YOUR DAY 15 WRITING PROMPTS

1. My father's voice still rings in my ears with messages of how to deal with death. He encourages me to not spend time living with resentment. What voices do you hear when you think about loss, or are facing the weight of regret?

2. Looking back with gratitude is a worthwhile exercise. Still, some stories cannot be changed. As we reflect, it's difficult to reconsider and remember people *only* with tenderness, especially if we know that we are not telling all parts of the story. What would you like to tell your blank page?

3. Gratitude helps us soften regret, and can nudge us forward. Interestingly, our resentments can tarnish our gratitudes. Think about some resentments you may be harbouring. Try nudging your grudges, and enjoy listing gratitudes for someone who is no longer living.

DAY 16:

CONDOLENCES PRECEDE THANKSGIVINGS, WORDS OF CHIEF JAKE SWAMP

My personal journals help me remember.

It was a surprise for me to find my journal entry dated July 9, 1994, reminding me of the time I attended a workshop, hosted by the Harmony Environmental Values Education Institute. I was among a group of people sitting on rocks that faced a sheltered bay on Vancouver Island, listening to the opening address delivered by Chief Jake Swamp of the Tree of Peace Society. The entire week proved to be exceptionally memorable for many reasons, but it was Chief Swamp who drove into our hearts a connection that I am only now able to fully embrace, almost 30 years later. I remembered that he opened our first day of conversations with a Prayer of Condolences, but without my notes, I would never have realized that he ended our first day with a Prayer of Thanksgiving.

Chief Swamp, according to my notes, expressed that "in order to bring our minds together as a family," we need to offer prayers to the spirit world—and we must remember to be grateful. My notes are an eye-witness account to his words and the address:

> *Harmony Opening Address: Chief Jake Swamp, Tree of Peace Society – Three condolences are shared whenever we come together as a group. Condolences to those who have lost loved ones.*

Tears blur our vision, so I will reach to heaven and find the softest skin of a fawn and I will wipe away your tears so that this week we will have clear vision.

When we suffer a loss, sometimes we lose our hearing. So, I will reach to heaven and wipe away the dust of your ears so we can listen to each other.

Sometimes when we grieve, we have a lump in our throat that makes it hard to speak. We lose our voice. So, I will reach to heaven and offer you a drink of clear water so that your voice will be restored and you can speak.

By offering condolences, we can find ways to help all people deal with their grief.

I know enough about memory to accept that I would never have remembered these exact words without my written record. I do, however, remember the lump in my throat, and tears welling in my eyes—my mind was not salved in that moment, but was locked in confusion, nervousness, anxiety and uncertainty.

My parents were still alive at that point, but I knew that the coming watershed event was not far off. As worried as I was for their decline, I was also consumed with worry for the future, and for my children's place in it. For good measure, thoughts of death and doom were swirling in my mind, and I nervously thought about the fate of our planet, along with the looming loss of people close to me.

My journal notes from that day go on for many pages, reminding me of Chief Swamp—his way of speaking, his posture as he sat on a big rock, his kind face, and the sparkle in his eyes as he encouraged us to overcome our anger, be happy, feel good about ourselves, and to always seek peace. His messages were about kindness, gratitude, sadness, valuing our children and planning for the future.

When this wise Elder spoke to us again that evening, he mentioned his writing project, committing to paper the Prayer of Thanksgiving. Knowing full well that his oral history tradition was being lost, Chief Swamp was confident of his message, but his confidence as a writer was tentative—he only had a ninth-grade education. He was apprehensive, but shared that he was working with an editor who was convinced that his words held power and needed to be saved.[24] While pursuing the process to generate a written document that would preserve his Prayer of Thanksgiving, this wise man spoke to our group from a voice that lay buried in the soil of his heart.

He delivered his prayer, often with his eyes closed. His soliloquy expressed intense gratitude for every life-sustaining force around us, seen and unseen: "When the world was new, we all came from the same place, the same source," he said. "We thank the Great Spirit first, and give thanks to Mother Earth, who supports our feet."

He continued by acknowledging all the gifts we have been given, including the Waters, Fish, Trees, Birds, Wind, and all of life's forces, including our Oldest Brother, "the Sun who never fails to show his face in the morning…and Grandmother Moon who controls the liquids inside us."

As he spoke, I wrote and kept my pen moving forward—a typical way for me to manage emotions when something powerful is brewing. A self-professed born-again pagan, Chief Swamp said that in his tradition, humans must first acknowledge our losses, and then return to a good spirit by giving thanks.

"When people grieve," he said, "we enter another state of mind. We keep trying to bring our griefs out. The minds of people who are close to those who have died keep their heads bowed with care."

He then told us of a dream he had. "A man came, and told me, 'Don't be afraid of death, for this is Nature. Everyone will experience it. When you see a person feeling the fear of death, take their hand, show them that water still flows in their veins. Trees still grow. The sun still shines.'"

Chief Swamp also posed a series of questions related to our roots. "Where are we from?" he challenged. "Who are we as people? Where do any of us really belong?" He spoke to the existential questions of our times—people from around the world were becoming more disconnected from the planet; we needed to look at the earth through a lens of collective engagement. Could we? Would we? Clearly, three decades later, answering these questions in the affirmative is even more pressing, if not dire.

"The most important thing," he assured us, "is to be in a good spirit when planning for our children's future. We need to instill in our children a feeling for their net worth." He added, "We are putting problems on the shoulders of youth. But we must support them so that they can make the changes."

Without my journal, I would have remembered fragments of the Prayer of Condolences, but the rest of the memory would be vague, and lack substantive content. Now, 30 years later, I can reread the entry, which concludes with an invitation to teach students that "when you go to collect water, look to see which way the current is flowing. Then, dip in and collect the water and go with the flow of the river. This symbolizes not going against the flow of Nature."

YOUR DAY 16 WRITING PROMPTS

1. Condolences first, thanks second. What do you think? Do you have a wise Elder whose voice rings in your head, and draws a link between loss and thanksgiving? If you were to write your own prayer of thanksgiving to an aspect of nature (whether a single tree or the whole planet, your favourite star or the entire Milky Way), what would you say?

2. As I researched the history of the Condolence Ceremony, I discovered that it was last used in 1794—exactly two centuries before I sat as a witness—during a treaty signing ceremony with George Washington. That timeframe puts my personal genealogical narrative back to a seventh-generation elder, just then entering the world in the vicinity of northern England. What about you? What was happening in your family story in 1794?

3. What does "go with the flow" mean to you today? What energizes you as you list your notes of condolences and thanks?

Day 16 notes

24 I was delighted to find on the internet, *Haudenosaunee, Thanksgiving Address: Greetings to the Natural World*, words to the greeting documented in its entirety, and provided courtesy of Six Nations Indian Museum, and the Tracking Project. A similar version of the prayer that I remember hearing Jake Swamp recite from memory is here: https://americanindian.si.edu/environment/pdf/01_02_Thanksgiving_Address.pdf.

DAY 17:

INVITE YOUR IDEAL TRAVELLING COMPANION TO SHARE YOUR HEAD SPACE

Check your own thoughts and negativity biases.

At the community foundation, I was frequently invited to ribbon cuttings and grand openings, especially if our organization had made a grant in support of the project, or had been named to receive a gift.

One evening, I attended a social event and presentation in a sporting goods store. During the event, a highly accomplished mountaineer told an inspiring tale of grit, mental resilience and physical fitness, illustrated with a series of beautiful slides. Dressed humbly in a fleece jacket and climbing sandals, he spoke about the transformative moments he experienced in a very lonesome, inaccessible and challenging place known literally as Shangri-La. The photos of a honeycomb network of high caves and places of past civilizations were impressive, but it was the final slide that riveted me. It included a quote from the Chinese philosopher, Lao Tzu:[25]

> *Watch your thoughts, they become your words. Watch your words, they become your actions. Watch your actions, they become your habits. Watch your habits, they become your character. Watch your character, it becomes your destiny.*

I hadn't expected such a profound and thought-provoking conclusion to this adrenalin filled presentation, and the words struck a significant chord. The need to consider our beliefs, thoughts and motivations as the starting point of every step on life's journey is a good way to plan any expedition.

Lao Tzu's reminder helped me remember that June Callwood's encouragement was to start with kindness, but also cautioned that top-down kindness—when gifts given or received put the needs of the top ahead of those of the base—is a disabling strategy. At the time, I was aspiring to help our organization find ways to be kind in a bottom-up manner. Slowly, I began to consider instances where I might be putting our organizational needs ahead of the needs of groups we were serving. What was the best type of kindness? Were we guilty of missing the mark?

Habits of mind can trigger a cascade of consequences. In that our thoughts rise from what's inside of us—our beliefs, inner voices, emotions and influences—the only way to stop the ensuing avalanche is to keep writing your way to safety.

The last slide hadn't even disappeared from the screen before I decided to commit to new ways of thinking. For one, I admitted to myself that I'd gotten into the habit of making side jokes—as if some cynical shadow was starting to etch its way out. No more of those. Instead, I would look for ways to embrace silence, or strike positive tones that aligned with what our work meant at the grassroots level—not worrying about how it looked from the top. After all, understanding the culture of community grant-making and endowment fund building was new to our village. More than anyone, I needed to find the right voice and approach as we tackled the trek to our own Shangri-La.

When I sat with the thoughts that were flooding my mind, I realized that many of my conflicted ideas had to do with money: earning, raising, saving and spending it. This myriad of conflicts was couched in a set of ecology equations: dollars for operations…dollars to be used per donor wishes…having too much money meant X, but too little meant Y… And what about the optics of power, balance, imbalance, sustainability and leadership?

Aware of a confluence of things like mission drift, organizational health, and the well-being of the community, I made some hard decisions that night, and soon began putting them into practice:

- Treating people as dignified individuals with rights and responsibilities means being respectful, trusting, co-operative and open-minded. The door swings both ways.
- The art, literature, words and opinions that repel me, or create tension may be the exact things I need to contemplate and wrestle with. June Callwood had alerted me to this idea.
- Emotions will flow. Belief systems and past experiences are relevant and personal.
- After the heat of any moment passes and emotions settle, it's important to sit with silence. It pays to revisit and decide who I want as my best travelling companions, and to consider what to embrace, accept, alter, integrate or reject.
- It is important to let the person or group doing the heavy lifting take charge.
- Professional insight and careful communications are essential.
- Money is one of the tools in our toolbox. It is not, however, the sole indicator of success, and is of no use if it's not helping us help others.

Helping and caring for others brings out the goodness in each of us. Such acts can also come with challenges, especially when the help that's offered does not truly align with needs.

It takes courage to make changes. It is also important to note that every change triggers some kind of loss—you can't change and stay the same. Paying attention and monitoring the steps you've taken, even the ones made in kindness, may need revision, according to the needs of the other side.

YOUR DAY 17 WRITING PROMPTS

1. Which travelling companions do you wish to keep in your head? Which voices would you like to take along as you navigate change? Name them, and give them room to write today.

2. Which companions would you like to be rid of? Name them too, then wish them *adios*.

3. Regarding the companions who stay with you: tell them what you are grateful for. Be as honest, open and direct as possible.

4. The concept of rewiring thoughts and habits means intentionally disconnecting our quick thoughts and deliberately searching for healthier, more enjoyable options. By letting go of one story, what can you forget? As you track the feelings of letting go, can you write in the direction of acceptance, moving away from resentment and regret?

Day 17 notes

[25] Lao Tzu (sometimes written as Laozi and Lao-Tze) was an ancient Chinese philosopher and writer. He is the reputed author of the *Tao Te Ching*, the founder of philosophical Taoism, and considered a deity in religious Taoism and traditional Chinese religions.

DAY 18:

OTHER WAYS OF REMEMBERING, INCLUDING SONGS AND SMELLS

As we age, some hardwired memories can still rise up, even as our cognitive abilities decline.

Plenty of triggers can fire memories. Photographs, ticket stubs, lines of poetry, or overheard conversations can send your mind backwards in time. In my experience, sounds and scents can also be volatile memory prompts.

Another privilege of my community work involved site visits, and witnessing the impacts of the grants we awarded—a true chance to see dollars in action. Two grants that come to mind both involved agencies seeking to improve the quality of life for residents in our local extended care facility. In both cases, I witnessed what I still consider to have been minor miracles brought on by music, smells and sounds.

The first occurred during an intercultural exchange program—the grant paid for young dancers, dressed in traditional regalia, to perform for residents in the hospital's extended care unit. The Elders who were living on reserve in the nearby community accompanied the dancers with a traditional prayer and sweetgrass smudge ceremony, acknowledging the spirits of forces seen and unseen. As the Elders spoke, mothers fussed over their young dancers' hair adornments, and provided finishing touches here and there.

The audience—residents, staff and visitors—sat in a circle, while dancers, drummers and singers animated the scene.

Suddenly, from somewhere far down the hospital corridor, a small woman, wrinkled and wearing moccasins on her stockinged feet, ran into the room, and stood at the edge of the space. Her eyes were bright, and her entire face beamed in a toothless grin. It wasn't that she was running late, or coming from another event. Instead, the smoke had wafted the memorable smell of sweetgrass, and the sounds had wakened her from the stupor of institutional sterility. Running into the room with urgency, she arrived at a memory of joy, and followed a comforting link to her past.

Staff members were stunned to see her completely engaged, enthralled and focused. As a full-time hospital resident, she carried the label *non-verbal pacer*. Later, an occupational therapist shared that he had never seen this woman stand so still and attentive, transfixed by her memory.

The second time I witnessed a miracle of memory on fire also occurred in the common room of the hospital's extended care unit. A professionally trained music therapist made weekly visits to the ward, thanks to our external funding. Her goal was to stimulate the living space with her shimmering voice and brightly tuned guitar.

A circle of six people sat beside a gentleman named Jack, who was belted into his wheelchair. His grey head was bent forward, almost touching his lap, and he seemed to be sleeping. The musical therapist optimistically placed some green St. Patrick's Day beads around Jack's neck, and put a green party hat on his head, encouraging him to wake up. He remained unresponsive.

The group began singing, tapping their toes and shaking various noise makers, as the musical therapist played guitar. She placed a shaker in Jack's hand, walked over to her sound equipment and said, "Okay Jack, this song is for you. It's the one you requested last time."

In a moment, Frank Sinatra's famous voice boomed into the room, and we all smiled in recognition of *New York, New York.* Then, as if nudged by some unseen force, Jack's eyes popped open. He raised his head and started shaking the rattle in his hand. The music wafted deep into his body and mind, bringing him back from wherever he'd been. He raised both arms in the air, keeping time to the beat, and his upper body began to sway as he beamed with joy.

Not all memories come from within. Many are triggered by what's around us. Sometimes we go looking for something specific, but ideas often find us when we are facing the opposite direction.

YOUR DAY 18 WRITING PROMPTS

1. What music brings a smile to your face and helps memories rush to mind? What songs often run through your head on their own? Consider starting a musical playlist you want to listen to when you are 90 years old. Add a quick list of gratitudes to explain why you want to return to these songs or lyrics.

2. What about scents? What aroma moves you into memory? If it is near you now, bring it closer, and breathe it in deeply. Follow your writing into the scent, and see where it takes you. Start by writing: "I love the smell of ____, because it reminds me of ____."

DAY 19:

GRATITUDE, LIFE PURPOSE AND WELL-BEING

*A gift by definition is something freely given.
Money, material or transactional gifts that come with
obligations pose a challenge.*

Wise Elders, ecologists, economists, psychologists and spiritualists know that our thoughts are critical pivot points between our inner truths and our outside voices and actions. During my years of writing myself into action, when I was feeling confused or indecisive, or looking to settle myself down, I would ask, "What are the big rocks I need to get into the jar?" And the second question was, "If those are my big rocks, how do I manage my time and energy, and get the right filters for my thoughts?"

The big rocks are the really important things that define you. They are your non-negotiables, core values, relationships, purpose and secret sauce that make you who you are. They are your reasons for getting up in the morning and putting one foot ahead of the other. In my life, even when it looked bleak, my husband and I agreed that money was a tool—one of the pieces, but not the main objective. His oft-repeated line that runs through our family narrative declares, "Because the last shirt doesn't have a pocket."

Money cannot make us happier. Instead, we are happier when we decouple money from the assumption that it will make us happy. We become temporarily happy when we buy the bright shiny object of our heart's desire, but with time, we keep looking for brighter, shinier, newer versions of yesterday's widget.

It strains our systems of thinking, and defies a certain logic to our modern ways of life. If happiness, health and well-being are good goals, and if we assume that money is our accepted route to happiness, then we are going to miss meeting our goals. We may get richer, but that metric does not reflect our levels of health, well-being, happiness or contentment. If money isn't the answer to our greater sense of purpose and meaning, then what is?

In 2015, Scott Barry Kaufman published a study asking questions related to well-being, and nurturing the character strengths we've discussed throughout this book. With a statistical approach, the study concludes that the top three character strengths most strongly correlated to well-being are: Hope, Gratitude and Love.[26]

The bottom three strengths correlated with well-being on the VIA matrix (from Day 3) are Prudence, Self-regulation and Judgement. (If you recall, these three strengths were part of Day 11's Deeper Dive writing prompt.) Interestingly, Humility, while considered a character strength, does not have a correlation with well-being, but I always consider it to be a good approach in most situations. Clearly, our personal well-being is tightly woven into our socio-economic, emotional and cultural fabric, and filtering our perspective through a lens that is hopeful, grateful and grounded in love sets us up for an even higher level of well-being.

Similarly, if we can discipline our thoughts and ask them to stop being overly judgemental or self-regulating—which I interpret as being too self-critical—we are on track for living happier and healthier lives. After all, our habits, including habits of mind, make significant differences in our lives. Toward that end, I suggest that we vigilantly encourage any self-loathing or disrespectful inner voices to step away, thereby inviting sweeter filters to our thoughts.

According to Kaufman, Gratitude and a Love of Learning are two of the best independent predictors of well-being. We must stay open-minded, keep learning and make new neural connections, while continuing to love ourselves and others, trending in the direction of a more grateful disposition.

As far as my own research has uncovered, there are no known toxic side effects to good gratitude that is heart-felt, authentic and true. Cheerful giving must hit the mark of giving a gift with no expectation of reward. A gift is a gift is a gift—end of story. Eventually, the heart processes the story and decides to pay it forward, and the giving beat goes on.

The dark side of gratitude may raise its head when a gift over-burdens a relationship with an excessive level of obligation. I have seen gratitude that could be considered toxic manifest as a contractual agreement. It's the kind of gratitude that puts the needs and wants of the giver ahead of those of the receiver. This can create a power imbalance, especially when the giver's gift implies some sort of reciprocity agreement, rather than a gift freely given in a spirit of benevolence. If the subtext to a gift is *I am giving you this, so that you must give or do something in return*, then we have a gift with strings. This defies the meaning of good gratitude, and the rules of gratitude may not apply.

Gifts, by definition, are given without expectation of reward. If you make or receive a gift with strings attached, or with significant obligations rising, you should ask, "Is this really a gift?" and exercise your gratitude accordingly. Not everyone wants a puppy.

If you give or receive a gift assuming you will reap a benefit or some form of repayment, where does it sit on the spectrum of gratitude and kindness, versus duty and/or obligation? If a gift given is disproportionately large for the size of the relationship, and risks spilling some of your big rocks out of the jar, you might want to check your gratitude-o-meter. Does this object help you feel a sense of wonder, thankfulness and appreciation for life? If the answer is *yes*, your personal gratitude-o-meter will be zinging with light and energy. If the answer is *not at all*, there may be another conversation rising—after writing about it in your journal.

YOUR DAY 19 WRITING PROMPTS

1. Have you felt saddled with a burden of duty after receiving a gift? What memories do you have related to gifts that brought you closer to your life's big purpose and joys? Have you ever received a gift that distracted or took you down a path of repayment and transactional thinking?

2. Material, experiential or emotional: how would you define your favourite type of gift? List five or more of them today, and write about the things that make them so special. You might start by writing, "Favourite gifts that I have received…"

Day 19 notes

26 Scott Barry Kaufman, 2015. "Which Character Strengths are Most Predictive of Well-being?" https://blogs.scientificamerican.com/beautiful-minds/which-character-strengths-are-most-predictive-of-well-being/.

DAY 20:

WHO CAN HELP YOU STAY YOUR COURSE? YOU CAN.

Our master strength: the capacity to be loved.
Yes—to be loved.

Back when I was growing my personal commitment to kindness and volunteering, and also nurturing and encouraging our little family, American psychologists were taking steps to turn the disease-based model of emotional health and well-being on its head.

In 1998, Dr. Martin Seligman, then the newly elected president of the American Psychological Association (APA), claimed that he was part of a "tectonic upheaval in psychology called positive psychology".[27] I only discovered this science recently, when I decided to probe the science of gratitude and its benefits at the community level in the time of COVID-19.

In his book, *Authentic Happiness*, Seligman tells his founder's story, his motivation for change, and why he revised his mission away from a disease model, preferring to focus on mental health and wellness. After working for many years in the laboratory, he decided that a shift in focus away from what was considered "learned helplessness" would be of greater service to more people.

Dr. Seligman details the moment when his change orders were galvanized. He was weeding in his garden with his five-year-old daughter beside him. She was dancing and singing, throwing weeds into the air. As a self-described goal-oriented gardener, Seligman was unhappy with the distraction, and yelled at his little girl, who stormed off. A few minutes later she was back, commanding that he pay attention to her. She issued a challenge: since she had successfully met her goal to stop whining, she insisted that her father stop being such a grouch.

Seligman took the words to heart. He realized that his daughter did not need him to be grumpy and overly critical. Rather, he saw that she would face a better future if he could help her develop her social intelligence skills, what some might call the window to her soul. The movement he envisaged would focus on positive feelings such as hope, life satisfaction and happiness—and shift the focus away from depression, anxiety and sadness.

"The positive emotions of confidence, hope and trust serve us best not when life is easy," Seligman writes, "but when life is difficult. In times of trouble, understanding and shoring up the positive institutions, institutions like democracy, strong family, and free press are of immediate importance." [28]

With scientific rigor, research, peer reviews and statistical analyses, scientists and psychologists like Seligman have shifted away from motivations that are symptoms of illness or disease, and are focusing on ideas that improve our well-being, happiness and life satisfaction.

For my work in the world at a hyper-local level, positive psychology is relevant, and has direct lines to how I understand our ecology as a family, with our myriad of relationships in civil society. Our positive institutions thrive when we have strong social units, starting with the family unit as a fundamental building block. When our systems are thriving, we have healthy interactions, a nourishing environment, good infrastructure, and a democratic spirit fuelled by generous and accepting attitudes toward others. Our strong social capital includes opportunities for bonding, linking and building bridges to others, helping our villages create inclusion, and increasing our cultural and religious understanding of *the other guy*. To paraphrase Seligman, it's our connections to others and our relationships that give life its meaning and purpose.

With better states of mind, our human relationships can improve. With improved self-awareness, individuals will feel better about themselves. With better understanding of personal strengths, people will better relate to others, and our social systems will help us flourish.

Following the publication of *Authentic Happiness*, Seligman revisited some of his theories in a book entitled *Flourish*, published in 2013. Rather than commit to happiness as a goal for his work, he expanded his theories, taking a broader view of well-being that aspires to a higher life purpose and meaning in relationship to others. This newer book embeds positive psychology in a theory of well-being, with a goal of increasing the levels of flourishing in one's life.

In the footnotes to *Flourish*, Seligman refers to the science when he writes: "The capacity to love and to be loved was the single strength most clearly associated with subjective well-being at age eighty." [29] Elsewhere, referring to loneliness as a disabling condition, especially for young adults, he shares that:

> "…social co-operation has been a driving force in the evolution of human behaviour. The converse of social co-operation is loneliness and the disease of loneliness is taking its toll on everyone these days. Loneliness, feeling unsupported, believing that nobody cares about you is stressful,

and causes a negative spiral downward, fueled by self-defeating behaviours."[30]

Gratitude is a remarkable mirror, compass and flashlight that can help alleviate the lonely feelings that can plague our lives. Our relationships with others matter, as do our social investments of time, energy and resources. Our choices and goals related to purpose, meaning and life satisfaction are contingent on our ability to love and to be loved. More than anything, we must allow ourselves to be loved, and start seeing ourselves in the interactive flow of energy as benefactors and beneficiaries. Doing so is the path to living in relationships.

The following chart summarizes some of the science that Seligman presents:

In order to flourish must have:	In order to flourish must have at least 3 of:	Lonely young adults are higher in[31]	Lonely young adults are lower in[32]
Positive Emotion	Self-esteem	Anxiety	Optimism
Engagement, Interest	Optimism	Anger	Social Skills & Social Support
Positive Relationships	Resilience	Negative Moods	Positive Mood
Meaning and Purpose	Vitality	Fear of Negative Evaluation	Extraversion
Achievement, Mastery	Self-determination		Emotional Stability
Health			Agreeableness
			Sociability

YOUR DAY 20 WRITING PROMPTS

1. If you haven't already taken the VIA test of Character Strengths, visit their website, register for a free account, and begin: https://www.viacharacter.org. Note your scores on the following (or refer to your scores from Day 11):

Gratitude ____   Love of Learning ____   Hope____

Prudence ____   Judgement____   Self-regulation ____

2. Thinking about your character strengths, write a note of appreciation to yourself for the gifts you bring into the world when you are playing to your strengths. Consider how you might influence a younger person in the role of a benefactor, helping to inspire future generations.

Day 20 notes

[27]   Martin E.P. Seligman. *Flourish: Visionary New Understanding of Happiness and Well-being.* United States. Atria Paperback, a division of Simon & Shuster, Inc. 2011. p. 1.

[28]   Martin E.P. Seligman. *Authentic Happiness: Using New Positive Psychology to Realize Your Potential for Lasting Fulfillment.* United States. The Free Press, a division of Simon and Schuster, Inc. 2002. p. xiii.

[29]   Seligman, *Flourish*, p. 276.

[30]   ibid, p. 276.

[31]   J.T. Cacioppo and W. Patrick, *Loneliness: Human Nature and the Need for Social Connection.* United States. W.W. Norton, 2008. as cited in Seligman, *Flourish*, p. 276.

[32]   ibid, p. 276.

DAY 21:

COMPETITION VS. CO-OPERATION

Good relationships are co-operative and full of reasons for good gratitude, no matter what the race results page says.

Is gratitude always gratitude? Not quite. The more I dig into the topic, the richer the conversation becomes. Gratitude may be considered a *trait* that's linked to your hard-wired disposition. Or, it may be a *state*, linked to a quick and fleeting emotion. Trait gratitude is not an attitude of gratitude, but rather a character strength—something that can be developed, practiced and used with skill. It is like a muscle that needs intentional training. When cultivated through a daily or consistent practice, trait gratitude has a profound impact on social relationships and personal well-being.

A familiar and recurring personal story for me, one that spun my emotional compass between gratitude and regret for more than 20 years, relates to parenting children who pursued excellence in high performance sports. Two of our children have competed at a world-class level as cross-country skiers, starting when they were very young.

While I know plenty about watching volleyball, high school rugby and mountain bike racing, my mastery as a professional observer of cross-country ski racing came during a career that spanned four Olympic Games cycles, with numerous highs and lows along the path. Torino was a high in 2006. Vancouver in 2010 was a low. Sochi in 2014 was one high, one low. Pyeongchang in 2018 offered some modest highs, but lots of gratitude.

When the children were younger, I often volunteered as a chauffeur, kitchen helper or race day cheerleader. Each post-race analysis became a story, a chance to listen deeply and try to understand the racer's perspective, and justifications for why they did or did not advance to the podium on any particular day.

Cross-country ski racing is an apt metaphor for life. The sport is a complicated, incremental journey of micro-decisions that have cumulative effects, compounded by chance. When considering the variables, some of them are within the athlete's control, but all of them are beyond that of a parent.

As a winter sport, the weather, wind chill, humidity, quality and age of the snow, air temperature and plenty more require professional assessment, far beyond my ken. With the insight and support of coaches, technicians and logistics staff, racers learn about their strengths and weaknesses, quality of equipment, and how to prepare their minds, bodies and souls for maximum performance on race day. It is a fundamental point to understand that the higher the goal, the greater the challenge—and the more compelling the need for strong support scaffolding.

On the start line, every racer naturally wants to reach a personal best. Making quick decisions based on the advice of coaches and trainers, they compete with extreme effort and best calculations. In the midst of it all, change happens in a heartbeat. Then, at the finish line, the race over, the athlete must take time, gain perspective, and feel the warm arms of their supportive safety networks, helping to ease the transition between results and expectations.

Over the years, I waited for the phone to ring, eager to hear about outcomes and results—either goals met, or hopes dashed. Every call could be a chance to share a moment of exhilaration, or to be there for when crocodile tears began to fall.

"I chose the wrong skis."

"We got the wax wrong."

"My goggles fogged up, and the visibility was so poor that I fell over the edge of the track."

"I took a wrong turn," happened more than once, sometimes because a volunteer was standing in front of the directional marker, or because the concentration was so focused, the racer became oblivious.

Sometimes the story went like this: "I took too much speed going into the corner and lost control. It was a complete yard sale." Other times, *the other guy* had taken too much speed and crashed into my chosen favourite. Either way, the result was the same, and disappointment meant there would need to be another calibration of the dial.

Of course, there were plenty of joyful moments of success and delight. They won races, and travelled to Switzerland, Poland, Norway, Italy, Russia, across Canada and elsewhere after meeting selection criteria. There were Olympic moments of exhilaration and disappointment—yet the story was never just about winning or losing.

Anecdotes that started with "I got lucky" would relate how things could have ended differently. Even during tears and the choking sound of a breaking voice, I learned to quietly listen, waiting for a chance to ask, "Did anything go right?" or "What did you learn for next time?" Sometimes, the story was about the coach who said, "You skied the first half of the course really well. Now, we just have to work on your finishing kick." Or, perhaps the race highlight was, "I was skiing with the lead pack for a bit. It was a thrill to be shoulder to shoulder with those guys. They're the best in the world. It was super exciting!"

In ski racing, success or disappointment was never reduced to the outcome alone. The racer's success or failure was always relative and contextual. There were always new lessons to learn, new challenges to face, and new obstacles to assess. In fact, I finally learned that the competition was not about winning. I watched with delight as my racers talked about the thrill of suiting up beside the best in the world, and the profound appreciation they felt for being in the company of excellence. Disappointments were inevitable. However, when you are trying to reach big goals, success is often a page that one turns quickly. After all, once you attain one stage of proficiency, there are new lessons to learn, and new goals to reach.

In my years of working in the community, the groups and people I worked with fussed and grieved, advanced and retreated, lamented and celebrated in a fashion similar to my racers. We pushed hard up some hills, and sometimes had to wait for more favourable conditions before moving forward. We needed to learn patience. Sometimes, we pushed when we should have pulled; other times, we worked against each other, rather than pull together. When it was time to recalibrate, we often simplified things. The usual strategy was to retreat and hunker down in our silos, comforting ourselves. A better, more courageous strategy would have been to find the time and energy to navigate the complex, difficult conversations about *doing better next time.*

Transformational ideas tend to rise when we listen intently, declare our reasons to be grateful and pay attention to what is happening around us. Every parent, sibling, relative or person in a relationship knows that no matter how grateful we feel, life can change in a heartbeat. The ring of a phone, a knock at the door, a bump on the head and our life story shifts from elation to desperation, happiness to worry, ecstasy to sadness. Being grateful does not immunize an individual from experiencing pain and anguish. However, good gratitude can help recalibrate your system after you've received a negative blow.

YOUR DAY 21 WRITING PROMPTS

1. Think of a time when things didn't turn out the way you were hoping. What happened? And what happened next? And then what?

2. List five things you love to do, whether alone or as group activities. Who are the people you love having along for the ride?

DAY 22:

SNAKES, LADDERS AND LADDERSHIP

By anchoring yourself with gratitude, you can face your fears and gain confidence.

When I was growing up, board games were a common way to pass an hour. Monopoly could go on for days, but Snakes and Ladders was a quick and mindless game for passing a pleasant afternoon with others. Mindless, but perhaps it holds some apt metaphors for life and growing older.

The object of Snakes and Ladders is to progress along the rows and be the first to cross the finish line. How? Players advance their coloured plastic markers by counting squares on the board, moving from start to finish. You take a turn, roll the dice, count the squares, and advance your plastic marker accordingly. Simple…except that chance plays a factor.

When your marker lands on a square that is at the base of a ladder, or the mouth of a snake, your fortunes shift. Either you are rewarded with a quick rise and move forward, or you plummet back along a snake's tail.

Ladders help you advance faster. Some ladders are long, others are short, but all ladders help you move ahead. Snakes, on the other hand, are problematic. If you land on a square that opens into the maw of a snake, you are demoted, sometimes several rows back, placing you farther from the finish line. Some snakes are short and the consequences are minor; others are very long, and you wind up going a far way down.

Writing a book, planning an expedition, reaching for stretch goals, parenting children, racing a race, growing a company, living in pain, processing the past, navigating life in times of COVID—it's almost like one tumultuous game of Snakes and Ladders. We get good news, followed by bad news. We get closer to our dreams, then get knocked off our pins.

Since the start of COVID, snakes have risen in the form of restrictions related to social rules, patterns of engagement, our working habits, holiday rituals and travel plans. Then came the ladders. With the news of a vaccine, we welcomed the chance to rise from the belly of the viral beast. Epidemiologists, scientists and health care professionals working in the system found ways to diagnose and treat patients more successfully. Networks of legislators and service providers offered the global population a vision that saw more people vaccinated, and a world that could begin its post-pandemic recovery.

Then the snakes of skepticism, misinformation and fear-mongering took us off the path. The virus itself played the role of a snake that kept shedding it skin, naturally mutating into strains that were even more contagious and pernicious. Striving to get beyond pandemic restrictions, the effort to get the vaccine into the arms of more people was the most highly urgent and recommended ladder, but as of this writing, the snake pit continues to hold great power.

Over the years, I have watched many races where good luck met great timing and excellent communication. An athlete who is well-rested, nourished, supported and prepared with an unshakable confidence holds magical power in her arms, legs and lungs. For any athlete, being in the zone or flow is akin to being on fire, completely focused and ready to face whatever. Still, no matter how well prepared an athlete is, there are times when some other variable, be it positive or negative—a force I named a *je ne sais quoi*—is at play, and the fairy tale shifts direction, or ends completely.

It's not all that different in the everyday, non-sports world. Physical and emotional exhaustion bring aches; fatigue sets in; new hassles arrive; the next bill needs to be paid. Sometimes, a jealous comment, or someone else's insecurity can pull us down. Tall ladders draw our attention, but the snakes and saboteurs threaten our momentum.

Relationships affect a ladder's stability. Friends, colleagues, faithful pets, places and family, whether birth, chosen or adopted, are strong influences. Knowing your reasons to be grateful, celebrating your strengths, and recognizing your limits can help you lean your ladder on the right wall, and extend it to the right height at the right time.

Another factor is trust. Can you trust yourself as you recover from exertion? Can you trust your response to change? After exertion or effort, can you rebalance and recover?

In every community, village and team, people stand on the shoulders of others. Your ladder represents your life circumstances. Some days, you may feel stable; other days, you wobble. Your place on the ladder is not necessarily reliant on talent, money, privilege, education or personal appearance. Again, a *je ne sais quoi*, as our friend *chance* plays a role. Perhaps a chance encounter, a new remedy, unexpected risks, or an ever-possible *act of God* in the form of flood or fire can cause a seismic shift in the landscape of a life.

If you are going for the big stretch goal, you need to make sure your supportive anchors and bolts are well placed. Big goals take big effort, and it pays to think about your support scaffolding ahead of time, in order to ready yourself for an inevitable twist or turn.

YOUR DAY 22 WRITING PROMPTS

1. We are each vulnerable to the whims of change. My best advice is to get grounded. Use your journal to assess your variables and situation, decide what matters most, and ask for help when you need it. As you hit your daily reset button, feel free to begin to begin again. Use your pen to find the kernels of truth that can steady your thoughts, clear your focus and help you move forward. What goal would you like to reach?

2. If your journal—and specifically, your growing list of gratitudes—is a kind of mental health insurance policy, how can it shore you up for the risks ahead? With honest insight, awareness and experience, your journal can be many things—a tough love friend, personal advocate, trainer, coach, etc. Play with the idea of snakes and ladders. What snakes are you hoping to avoid? What advice would your coach like to give? Is this advice firm, gentle, energizing or overwhelming?

3. With gratitude, acknowledge a solid five anchors (people, places or things) that can help you stay centred when the winds of change shift.

DAY 23:

WHAT STORY DO YOU WANT YOUR MONEY TO TELL?

Change means knowing about your waters.

There is a story that many change agents use, when advocating for a system's review: two fish are about to swim past each other, but decide to pause for a casual hello. The first fish says to the second, "Hi! How is the water?" And the second fish, a little confused, stops, looks around and asks in return, "What's water?"

The point is that if we want to talk about change, and specifically positive change, we first need to understand the waters in which we are swimming. And there's a second point as well—we need to talk to each other. Then, with insight and conversation, we gain an understanding of the other person's perspective, and can begin to consider ways of doing things differently, and hopefully better.

Water, as a life-sustaining force on our blue planet, is a powerful metaphor for our world and reality. When we see ourselves as separate from our environment, and parse our various ecosystems into silos—emotional, historical, cultural, socio-economic or political—we risk missing the point. Our silos of thought function as part of a larger, interconnected system, which itself exists within a network of other systems.

When we decide something needs to change, we may be reluctant to talk about it, even if the reasons for change seem obvious. Perhaps we're afraid that by talking about it, we will expose ourselves and our vulnerabilities. A personal journal can help you understand your water and vital sources.

One mental model that can be a significant stumbling block for people, myself included, involves our relationship to money. Having worked in the gift economy, I was committed to a vision that valued a culture of kindness beyond financial metrics. By expanding our networks of silos locally and regionally, investing in good social capital projects, building positive relationships, answering the phone with smiles in our voices, and paying attention, we showed up as agents of good in community spaces. Once people knew more about our work, we reasoned, they would learn to trust us. With trust, our credibility would rise, dollars would flow, and our philanthropic relevance would continue to grow.

I am happy to use the word philanthropy when it refers to practical acts of kindness, and gifts freely given in service to others. However, when philanthropy is defined with a narrow, elite view of "people with deep pockets who hold the power and know how to get things done," some good ideas might get an excellent kickstart, but it's not enough to guarantee a project's success. Without talented allies, and an understanding and deep respect for social, local, cultural and ecological stories, every good idea risks failure.

When the markets dropped in 2008, and the value of our organizational endowment fund sat below its cost-value watermark—thereby showing a loss on our year-end statements—it made me very sad to see how much energy was spent worrying about *the numbers*.

Too much focus went to asking questions and devoting nervous energy to the performance and *perceived value* of our endowed investments. These factors were far beyond my control—not my area of expertise or part of my career motivation. I was willing to trust our team of advisors, including accountants, investment counsel, fund managers and professionals who had been legally engaged to help us adhere to the laws of the land. We followed our policies, and stayed within our legal context and mission related to the greater good—we ran programs that benefited our community. The investments in our portfolio were influenced by systems far removed from my fishbowl.

As for cash, I knew how to steward real dollars in the here and now. As part-owner in the family business, I understood the relationship between revenue and expenses. Our bookkeepers paid close attention to the bank balance as we monitored our watermarks and worked hard to stay afloat.

Around this time, I discovered Lynn Twist's book, *The Soul of Money*, and shouted "Hallelujah!" out loud. The dust jacket describes Ms. Twist as a veteran global activist and fundraiser, and the contradiction of her book's title quickly grabbed my attention.

The book simplified for me the conflicted world views about money that were pounding me down. As Twist writes, money was invented to facilitate the sharing and exchanging of goods and services among individuals and groups. "For most of us," she writes, "this relationship with money is a deeply conflicted one and our behaviour with and around money is often at odds with our most deeply held values, commitments and ideals—what I call our soul."[34]

I read and underlined this passage:

> "There is little that we accept so completely as the power and authority of money, and assumptions about how we should feel about it. We challenge assumptions about every other facet of life: race, religion, politics, education, sex, family, and society. But when it comes to money, we accept it not only as a measure of economic value but also as a way of assigning importance and worth to everyone and everything else in the world. When we talk about success in life, money is almost always the first, and sometimes the only, measure we use for it."[35]

As for the soul, Twist defines it not as a religious interpretation, but rather as: "the things we choose to believe in, what deeply matters to human beings, *our most universal soulful commitments and core values,* is the well-being of the people we love, ourselves and the world in which we live."[36]

Lynn Twist helped me revise my relationship with money. Rather than see it as a necessary evil, money could be used for soul work, as an expression of joy, and social currency for investing in the well-being of the people we love, and the world in which we live. It is a tool for helping others and ourselves to flourish.

YOUR DAY 23 WRITING PROMPTS

1. In another book, *The Seven Stages of Money Maturity*, author George Kinder refers to "money maturity," suggesting that once we resolve our inner conflicts related to money, we can gain a sense of ease. As you get started with your writing today, consider the conflicts that money sets up in your soul. Where are these from? Are they yours alone, or

did you inherit them? Where does your writing take you as you explore your relationship with money? Can you think of ways that money can be more humanizing and of greater benefit for all?

2. Day 23 gratitude tracking: make a list of five things you are grateful for, starting each statement "I am grateful for…"

Deeper dive: As you consider your money maturity in relation to that which Ms. Twist calls your soul—the things that matter most to human beings—how does your view of the landscape shift? Think about how you invest your time and money by referring to the Adding Some Soul to Your Values activity found on page 188.

Day 23 notes

[34] Lynn Twist, with Teresa Barker. *The Soul of Money: Reclaiming the Wealth of Our Inner Resources.* United States. W.W. Norton & Company. 2003. p. 11.

[35] ibid, p. 9.

[36] ibid, p. 11.

DAY 24:

JOIN ME IN IMAGINING...

Good thought leadership strengthens our social capital
and communal unity.

When I was a youngster, my mother was always quick to pull out her trusty type-written list of names and phone numbers, flip the page and dial around for village helpers— friends who would bake pies or bring flowers for a baptism, funeral or wedding. Sure enough, Mildred, Doris or Melba would respond in a heartbeat. In other villages, some people see no need for home insurance, because they know that their neighbours will rally with know-how and materials if a structure or roof needs repair or replacing. In traditional hunter-gatherer villages, community freezers are packed full of fish or venison, available for families whose hunters come home late, or empty-handed.

A helping culture is not specific to Canada, but it *is* specific to creating a visionary culture that seeks community abundance. The Filipino word *bayanihan* expresses the idea perfectly—it refers to communal unity, and the desire to help others without expectation of reward. Community is, at its heart, about sharing our common destiny as human beings.

"Join me in imagining our country as it could be," the Right Honourable David Johnston said to a crowded room in 2011, "...a smart and caring nation, where all Canadians can succeed, contribute, and develop their talents to their fullest potential."

This call to action was direct, inclusive and inspirational, delivered by a man who was a thought leader and role model for Community Foundations of Canada. As he stepped away from the podium that morning, my tablemates and I clapped with enthusiasm, inspired by the positive endorsement inherent in our work, and grateful for the encouragement to continue our work in community with a commitment to being kind while putting good thoughts into action.

By acknowledging and reminding us of small-town values that teach us to support each other in neighbourly ways—and to trust each other in case the unexpected occurred—our hearts and souls were ignited. The idea of being part of a national network that was co-creating dreams of possibility, positivity and good vibrations sent the hairs on the back of my neck zinging.

Back then, I was six years into my job, leading an organization that wanted to connect the dots between hearts, heads, hands and yes, open pocket-books. From local priorities to national responsibilities, realities on the ground to pie-in-the-sky visions, we were patiently encouraging a culture of philanthropy that needed donations of time, talent and treasure.

At the micro, individual-to-individual level, good leaders acknowledge that people can offer various gifts, based on their personal circumstance, and that gratitude, in essence, is a tremendously personal motivator. Planning gifts to serve our communities in smarter, more caring ways meant that we needed to convene conversations that were relevant, respectful, inclusive, uplifting and inspirational. The language, tone, timing and intent all mattered.

Good thought leadership inspires action, and helps set our collective sights on higher goals. When we trust that our leaders are moving us along the right course, we become more productive and optimistic. When we are energized and aligned, and when systems are in place to support us, we can do good things better. Can you envision a staircase or ladder leading upward?

Looking at the practical side of community leadership, things can get messy, and feel overly iterative. It requires skill, patience, perspective and persistence when trying to corral people who find inspiration from a diversity of sources, messages and messengers. If a message resonates, leaders in the community philanthropic sector have the potential to strengthen our collective purpose—inspiring us to increase our efforts by working in the context of a greater common goal. Or, they can focus only on material concerns, and miss reconciling a bottom line that is benevolent, fairer and more just.

With vision, community efforts can open doors for citizens who want to offer their talents in service to a higher purpose. When groups play to their strengths with principles of inclusion, acceptance and co-operation, rather than strictly competition, there is good reason to celebrate collective achievement.

Even small wins can be savoured, especially when they ripple outward from gratitude. Good leaders encourage and inspire us to take micro-mini steps as part of a collective movement in the direction of building a world with more grace.

YOUR DAY 24 WRITING PROMPTS

1. Look around your village, office, team, etc. Who are your thought leaders with good ideas that can energize the story with positivity?

2. Here's a challenge: silence the voices in your life that do not inject your days with joy. Make a plan to unsubscribe, unfollow or unleash your tether from leaders, writers or influencers who are eager to inspire negative or destructive thoughts.

3. Think about one person, be it a thought leader, role model or mentor, who has influenced your life positively. Make a list of five things you would like to tell this *gratitude influencer* over a meal one day.

DAY 25:

GRATITUDE AND SYSTEMS CHANGE

Beliefs that limit and cause us to cling may need
some insight and faith.

If we base our aspirations for change in the direction of positivity—even if we only manage to nudge the needle a few millimeters—gratitude is never a weakness. And, it should certainly never be dismissed as being somehow too emotional, soft or insignificant. In its most powerful form, gratitude is a way to recalibrate conversations and reinforce connections. With gratitude, you can crystallize your thoughts related to the things that matter most to you.

In the early days of my morning journal practice, I read a book called *The Wisdom of Insecurity* by Alan W. Watts. As I read and reflected, I underlined Watts's wisdom as he explained how "brain thinking" was dominating our lives, rather than "instinctual wisdom." According to Watts, we are at war within ourselves, in part because we are concerned for the future, which only exists in our brains. He writes:

> "...we become totally frustrated, for trying to please the brain is like trying to drink through your ears...Happiness then, will consist, not of solid and substantial realities, but of such abstract and superficial things as promises, hopes and assurances."[37]

Written in 1951, the book explores the contradictory relationship between science and religion—between fact, metaphysics, mystery and emerging theories. In Watts's view, science had become the predominant authority in the minds and imaginations of the masses. Skepticism in spiritual matters and religious dogma posed a challenge to personal belief systems. "Belief clings, but faith lets go," he writes, suggesting in his argument that faith is indeed the main virtue of science as well as any religion that is not self-deception.

Around this same point in my life, I also read *The New Drawing on the Right Side of the Brain*, in which author Betty Edwards explains that the human brain uses two fundamentally different modes of thinking.[38] While both sides process data, Edwards points out that the brain's left hemisphere is built to process verbal, analytic, *sequential* data, while the right deals with visual, global, *perceptual* information. In other words, there are indeed two sides to every thought, word and idea, as our brains work overtime across two hemispheres. (Lucky for me, I can justify my tendency to contradict myself…I have two minds at work!)

Reconciling emotions, motives, thoughts and actions has long been a personal obsession, especially as I have navigated worlds of systems, relationships and memories, and my relationship with the past, present and future.

Do you remember our fish from Day 23? Well, here they come again. The first rule of being a fish: enjoy swimming in the waters to which you are best adapted. If you aren't in the right water, consider some new options, rather than clinging to old beliefs. You might choose to change your water, swim upstream, swim near the surface, dive deeper, or expand beyond your shore. You might want to consider a change of profession, career path, school or team. You may even gain the courage to change some unwavering opinion you've held forever.

Bringing Watts back into the equation, he advises that we cannot use our beliefs for hanging on to life. We cannot understand the mystery if we are busy trying to grasp and cling to the waters running downstream. There is a moment where the best thing we can do is to let go and have faith in the *je ne sais quoi* that awaits.

Now, for the first rule of gratitude: it *is* personal, and you have to figure it out for yourself. You may have to go back, assess past experiences, or scrub away some scabs and limiting beliefs in order to reveal the mysterious, valuable and meaningful gifts that are full of potential.

As you look backwards, remember the first rule of revisiting the past: leave hitch-hikers behind. Those ideas and memories that pop out of the shadows and seem somewhat dangerous are best left on the side of the road.

And of course, remember the first rule of writing: be patient. In that you've arrived at Day 25, you clearly have been patient with yourself. Now, as you think about your next steps and personal change plan, be kind, and do no harm—especially to your inner child, or to any child that is hiding in the soul of another person.

YOUR DAY 25 WRITING PROMPTS

1. What if you took a *wisdom of insecurity* approach to your thinking, feeling, living and writing—one that isn't trying to be too smart, skeptical or overly confident? What changes for you when you trend toward acceptance and tolerance for the many contradictions of life?

2. Going further, what beliefs are you clinging to? What leaps of faith can you take when you consider others? Can you accept that everyone has personal strengths that make them unique—maybe even a bit quirky and full of contradiction? Can you make space and accept your own quirks in the process?

3. Working from the light of positivity and hopeful possibility, how can you become less critical of weaknesses and inconsistencies—your own, and those of others? As you conclude your writing, consider the waters in which you are swimming. Compose a list of gratitudes that can stimulate ideas for paddling or swimming more capably, as you prepare for the next set of rapids, eddies, waves and troughs.

Day 25 notes

[37] Alan W. Watts *The Wisdom of Insecurity: A Message for an Age of Anxiety.* United States. Pantheon Books, a division of Random House Inc. 1951. p. 24.

[38] Betty Edwards. *The New Drawing on the Right Side of the Brain: A Course in Enhancing Creativity and Artistic Confidence.* United States. Jeremy P. Tarcher/Putnam, a member of Penguin Putnam Inc. 1999. p. xvii.

DAY 26:

THE CHALLENGE—GO BACK SEVEN GENERATIONS

Accept the challenge of living into your legacy.

On June 11, 2008, Canadian Prime Minister, Stephen Harper, delivered a formal apology to a special joint session of the House of Commons and the Senate. Harper's apology was another step in a multi-year process involving churches, governments, communities and First Nations peoples across Canada that continues today.

The 2008 apology was arranged by the government and representatives of the First Nations, and was one step in an ongoing attempt to address the government's role in the history of the Indian Residential Schools. The apology began:

> "Mr. Speaker, I stand before you today to offer an apology to former students of Indian residential schools. The treatment of children in Indian residential schools is a sad chapter in our history... Today, we recognize that this policy of assimilation was wrong, has caused great harm, and has no place in our country...

> "The government now recognizes that the consequences of the Indian residential schools policy were profoundly negative and that this policy has had a lasting and damaging impact on aboriginal culture, heritage and language."[39]

About this time, I was having lunch with a prospective donor named Pat, when the topic of the apology came up. We both agreed that it was high time to move the needle on policy changes that would help to create a more just and positive future for our Indigenous neighbours. We wondered aloud if the apology would make any difference.

"I sure hope so," we echoed each other. It was fitting that Pat and I were meeting, because she and I had been talking about legacy gifts, and discussing the technicalities of naming a charitable organization in her will. At one point she asked, somewhat rhetorically, "Because, it's all about legacy, isn't it, Lorraine?"

I was clinging to the belief that building relationships and working with others at the community level—co-ordinating our views of what could be done—would help our educational, cultural and socio-economic systems move in the direction of greater equity and access. While our specific geographic region didn't directly include members of the Stoney Nakoda Nation living on the reserve at Morley, 40 kilometers to the east, our public school board supported students and families living on those adjacent lands. Some of our school programs were intended to help bridge gaps, build inter-cultural understandings, and encourage friendships—such as the dance that I witnessed and described on Day 18.

Fast forward to the summer of 2015. I had been invited to a ceremony, paying witness to the signing of the Buffalo Treaty.[40] Motivated to work on projects that could help to right some historical wrongs, and simultaneously improve the integrity of our local ecosystem, the Treaty was the culmination of a multi-year, multi-stakeholder, multi-jurisdictional initiative that would re-introduce bison to a remote valley in the Canadian Rockies in the years to come.

At that point, I had only a limited understanding of the profound significance of this program, but I knew that Parks Canada, the federal agency behind the program, was methodically working with numerous stakeholders, thought leaders, band leaders, Elders and people with significant cultural ties to the buffalo. It was another complex web of relationships, and an ecology that wove together a myriad of social, historical, cultural, economic, environmental and legislative strands.

At the signing, Indigenous leaders, politicians, ecologists, and thoughtful experts from a range of disciplines penned their names on a treaty that would guide the return of the extirpated buffalo to its traditional lands. "The buffalo," one kind Elder explained, "is like our grocery store. It is our Walmart. The buffalo can give us everything we need—hide, horns, meat, bones…it is synonymous with survival."

In a long, sad story of broken trust, the event was a quiet moment that signalled some new beginnings. All around us, I could feel the ebb and flow of tension, excitement, anticipation and wariness. Once the formal ceremony ended, I stood alone, taking stock of the day's importance and watching the crowd drift away. I smiled as a man walked past me, and, admiring the traditional beading of his fringed buckskin jacket, said hello.

He turned, asking, "Where are you *from*?" I suddenly felt awkward. It wasn't a friendly or innocent question, and I wondered how to answer as words like *colonizer* and *settler* filled my brain.

"Oh, I'm from Banff," I finally said.

His nostrils narrowed and his lips tightened as he looked me straight in the eye.

"You're not *from* Banff. I mean where are you *really* from? Your relatives." His dark eyes held mine with razor sharpness as he continued sternly. "You need to go back and find out where you are *really* from. And I mean seven generations back."

He abruptly turned, scuffed the ground with his boot and walked on. I stood speechless, watching the sway of his fringe as he receded from view.

Like most people, my past is indeed full of open memories and flash points. Plenty of conversations remain unresolved. Along with my occasionally shoddy or selective memory, and my many personal biases, it took a long time for me to find the energy to look for some resolution to this challenge. This encounter can still bring tidal waves of emotions, punctuated with guilt, regret and shame. The point, as experts advise, is not to stay stuck in any memory, but to find ways to plod through and try to break free.

Our brains have evolved in such a way that we are constantly scanning for threats and keeping our guards high. When we feel threatened, we concentrate on things that we fear, or that make us uncomfortable. Looking back at this encounter, I wonder if my presence at the signing ceremony triggered a threat in this man's brain. Our biases, labels and world views may put us at odds with each other, but when we make sweeping generalizations, we may also be clinging to limiting beliefs, forgetting that the word kindness has two sides in every story.

As usual, I used my journal to embroider my side of the story. I obsessed, ruminated, defended myself and wondered what I could have said that would have been kind, insightful, helpful or explanatory. I knew that silence had been my best answer:

Morning Journal - September 1, 2015 – It is part of our Canadian identity to be kind, to care, to help others and to invest in our own self-development. To aspire and bring our friends and families along with us. To accept responsibility for ourselves and feel confident that should the need arise or the winds of change blow hardship our way – a safety net of support, a smart and caring blanket of community kindness will appear. I pray that some of the threads in that blanket can be found right here in our offices...

YOUR DAY 26 WRITING PROMPTS

1. Take a look at your writing from Day 14. The prompt, encouraged by Dr. Seligman, is a chance to stop over-emphasizing bad experiences. "Gratitude amplifies the savouring and appreciation of the good events gone by," he shares, "and rewriting the history by forgiveness loosens the power of the bad events to embitter (and actually can transform bad memories into good ones)."[41] Is now a good time to recast or reframe some past event? Can your gratitude practice loosen or shift some powerful feelings? Has your resolve hardened in any direction?

2. Can hope play a role in the context of an open memory? Czech playwright, dissident and activist Vaclav Havel writes: "Hope is definitely not the same thing as optimism. It is not the conviction that something will turn out well, but the certainty that something makes sense, regardless of how it turns out."[42]

3. What are you hoping for?

4. In her lyrical poem, Emily Dickinson sings her praise for hope, by writing, circa 1861:

"Hope is the thing with feathers
That perches in the soul –
And sings the tune without the words –
And never stops – at all…"[43]

Does your memory have a hope that has been wordlessly singing?

Day 26 notes

[39] Source: https://www.facinghistory.org/stolen-lives-indigenous-peoples-canada-and-indian-residential-schools/historical-background/prime-minister-harpers-apology. The Canadian Constitution recognizes three groups of Aboriginal peoples: Indians (more commonly referred to as First Nations), Inuit and Métis. These are three distinct peoples with unique histories, languages, cultural practices and spiritual beliefs. Source: https://www.national.ca/en/perspectives/detail/no-perfect-answer-first-nations-aboriginal-indigenous/.

[40] The agreement stemmed from proposals to bring free-ranging bison back to the areas like Banff National Park, aiming to restore links that existed when bison roamed free throughout the territories of the signatories. "Historic Treaty Signed Among 10 First Nations and Tribes in Banff." Posted August 14, 2015. https://www.cbc.ca/news/canada/calgary/historic-treaty-signed-among-10-first-nations-and-tribes-in-banff-1.3190715 Accessed 2 September 2021.

[41] Martin E.P. Seligman, *Authentic Happiness: Using New Positive Psychology to Realize Your Potential for Lasting Fulfillment*. United States. The Free Press, a division of Simon and Schuster, Inc. 2002. p. 70.

[42] From: https://www.brainyquote.com/quotes/vaclav_havel_392717.

[43] From: https://www.litcharts.com/poetry/emily-dickinson/hope-is-the-thing-with-feathers.

DAY 27:

THE RESPONSE—WITH HELP FROM UNCLE HUGH

Family can help recalibrate your place on the compass.

The challenge I received the day of the treaty signing—a demand that I go back seven generations to find out where I'm *from*—set me back emotionally, and it took some time to recalibrate. My writing from the next morning is full of worry:

> *Morning Journal - They say that the body remembers blood lines and all of our traces of being in a time prior to the here and now. I wonder... The defiant snarl of a buttery skinned brown-eyed warrior has me wondering about my blood lines. His question "where are you from?" puts me on a collision path with my past. I am afraid to go back. What if I find things that make me uncomfortable? What if I am complicit in something I knew nothing about? What if...*

The provocation stuck in the back of my mind like a thorn, where it festered. The words struck a nerve, and I knew that, at some point, I would have to accept the challenge. If I wanted to see this man through a lens of kindness, shared humanity and compassion, I needed to do some research. Lucky for me, I discovered a gentle time-traveller in the family who helped me find a positive affirmation in the shadows of my backwaters.

On the side of Dorothy Esther Guthrie, my mother, our roots were long, sunk deep into the farmlands of southern Ontario. The Guthrie-Smith links connect me to United Empire Loyalists, and the rolling hills of Scotland. On this side, I come from a line of people who were likely peasants and serfs, wanting to escape feudalism. They settled as hard working farmers and formed the backbone of early *Canadiana*. But what about my father's distant strands of DNA that lived in my cells?

I remembered seeing a pile of small leather diaries in a musty cupboard in the basement of our family home. My father's mother, Grandma Carson, born Hesba Pedley, was the daughter of Methodist minister Charles Stowell (CS) Pedley. Grandma's father had a famous brother, Uncle Hugh, and his diaries were the ones in the basement.

Online, I found mention of Mr. James Pedley. Born in 1820, this family member was seven generations back, and lived in northern England. He was an engraver by trade, and was part of a family legacy of writers, ministers, missionaries, orators and citizens who became minor characters in Canada's young history of social reform.

My online research led me to a paper written by Canadian historian Mélanie Méthot. In her Ph.D. thesis, Méthot shares that Reverend Hugh Pedley, my father's great-uncle, was a social activist in the first quarter of the 20th century. [44] Over his lifetime, Hugh travelled back and forth between England and Canada, and spoke from the pulpit in Winnipeg and Montreal. As a child, he lived in impoverishment, surviving on turnips the winter his mother died. His father, Charles Pedley, was also a socially conscious thinker, and a preacher who penned a well-received history of Newfoundland. Writing in the 1860s, this relative who lived five generations prior to me would have been a contemporary of Charles Dickens, the influential novelist who drew attention to the plight of child labourers, poor working conditions, social injustices and income inequities in England. I like to ponder whether the two

Charles's would have met in some literary setting, more than a century and a half ago.

Returning to Uncle Hugh, writing in Canada at the time of The Great War, his faith-based teachings and convictions put him in a moral camp that adamantly opposed the scarlet sins. Hugh saw a better world for all—once alcohol, prostitution and gambling were eradicated. In a 1915 sermon delivered from a Montreal pulpit, he declared:

> "There are three facts in human nature that stand in the way of the regeneration of society and these are: Ignorance. Sloth. And Selfishness."[45]

As a recognized influencer in Canadian church history, Uncle Hugh's faith informed his social conscience. He contributed to a public discourse that wanted to show how profit-oriented entrepreneurs were endangering the physical, mental and moral health of citizens.[46] He spoke out against market forces that promoted individualism and self-interest with no regard to others, and his ideals of social reform preferred a collectivist social order—something he called communitarianism—in opposition to the growing population of urban elite.

Uncle Hugh's ultimate and ideal solution to rectifying our social vices called for Congregationalist, Methodist and Presbyterian churches—three distinct protestant denominations—to unify and work together. This became the focus of his life's work. While Hugh died two years before The United Church of Canada was officially recognized, the records indicate that his commitments of time, passion and focus were influential in the discourse that led to unification.

Uncle Hugh's larger concerns were spiritual rather than political or economic. He saw the tension that existed between the needs of society, and those of the individual, especially concerning rights and freedoms. He was part of a movement that pointed fingers at the economic waste that came from competition, greed and selfishness, and noted the unequal distribution of the world's wealth—issues that continue to plague our global village several generations later. He denounced sectarianism and rebuked the hatred that pits nation against nation. He favoured universal education, moral enlightenment, temperance and a utopian ideal that would benefit humankind.

In an attempt to understand the times and culture of Canada from those days, I did more reading. There are various printed records that note an interesting and coincidental paradox: as the number of commercial elites and businesses began to rise, so too did Canada's burgeoning philanthropic and charitable culture. On one hand, observers noted the growth of urban life that some considered a depersonalization of services; on the other, groups were forming to address the physical, social and moral needs of a new class of urban poor.

As I acted upon the challenge I'd been handed, my thoughts gained focus. I put names to ideas, which helped me straighten out the wires of my personal belief system. I also continued to chew on a list of swirling questions: Whose job is it to move the needle on badly needed social reforms? Should the work fall to the church? The state? Is the work best done by charitable organizations fuelled by corporate funds, or should big business take a lead? Are these options best framed as *either/or* scenarios, or can they exist in the world of *and/also* thought leadership?

Méthot writes in her thesis that while social gospellers were focused on social vices:

"They were fighting the political machines and their con-
comitant corruption, abuses of power as well as patronage…the value of ideas is derived from the social context
from which they emerge." [47]

Uncle Hugh and others were fighting the corruption that accompanied political machines in their formative years. The
collective work of the gospellers positively influenced the
discourse of early Canadian society. They advocated for educational reforms and women's suffrage, and pointed to the
importance of urban planning, access to clean water, sewage
treatment, transportation, roadways, public ownership and
land conservation. And, they paid close attention to the rising
tension between individual freedoms and society's needs.

Thought leaders like Uncle Hugh were asking some big questions that continue to ring today, including one of particular
resonance: "Why leave to charity what is a human right?"

Once the serious threats to the soul, namely gambling, prostitution and intemperance were addressed, Uncle Hugh envisioned that the church would have a greater social function—
becoming more than just a place of worship. A newspaper
of the day described Hugh as "a man who thinks, who faces
vexing questions squarely, who does not avoid the sometimes
unorthodox solutions, and who expresses his opinions, ortho-
dox, or unorthodox, with a fearless tongue." [48]

YOUR DAY 27 WRITING PROMPTS

1. Do you have some famous or infamous characters in
   your past? Can you use the lens of gratitude to guide
   your exploration?

2. Investing in an appreciative inquiry about my past has allowed me to say goodbye to certain voices, and consider new doors to a future based in self-awareness and acceptance. With gratitude, I more readily close the doors I no longer need, and embrace the notion that life is full of contradictions. What doors can gratitude help you close or open today?

3. In his 1915 sermon, Hugh Pedley said, "Imagine this world peopled by a race of human beings who were intelligent, full of energy, and animated by love. Would it not be a good world to live in?"[49] What do you think about the phrase *animated by love*? If we love something, we are grateful for it. How might your past be shaping your future?

Here are a few of my gratitudes, based on my family research:

- I am grateful for the hard work of my predecessors: farmers, physicians, ministers, writers, social activists, thought leaders and caring teachers.
- I am grateful for people working to make change and looking for ways to do things better.
- I am grateful for the people who served in our wars, and people who tried to address the needs of women and children, outcasts, and of those who fell on hard times in a system that kept them in poverty and despair.
- Mostly, I am grateful for the decent people who faced huge challenges in every corner of our history. It's possible that my DNA is also lined with the efforts of scoundrels and wags, but I choose to believe that they too were trying to do the best they could, given the tools, training and oil lamps at their disposal, while facing down fears that haunted their nights.

Day 27 notes

[44]   Mélanie Méthot, *Social Thinkers, Social Actors in Winnipeg and Montreal at the Turn of the Century*. A Thesis Submitted to the Faculty of Graduate Studies in Partial Fulfilment of the Requirements for the Degree of Doctor of Philosophy, Department of History; University of Calgary, 2001.

[45]   "War and the New Earth," a sermon preached by Reverend Hugh Pedley, D.D. in Emmanuel Congregational Church, Montreal. Sunday Evening. May 30, 1915. United Church Archives. Méthot papers.

[46]   Mélanie Méthot. *Forgotten Social Gospellers: Reverend J.B. Silcox and Hugh Pedley*. Historical Papers, 2002; Canadian Society of Church History.

[47]   Méthot, *Social Thinkers, Social Actors*...pp. 12; 26.

[48]   Méthot, *Social Thinkers, Social Actor*...p. 233.

[49]   "War and the New Earth," Méthot papers.

DAY 28:

THE GRATITUDE LETTER—
THE MOST PROFOUND PRACTICE

Experiencing and validating the science and power
of the gratitude letter.

If I had followed a career in ecology, I would have wanted to
spend a good portion of my time in the field, on the ground,
and out in the natural world, rather than in the laboratory
or library. That way, I could be in touch with the real world,
able to test my ideas, and verify everything I was trying to
communicate by ground-truthing the scientific theory. The
same holds true for this 30-day journey of writing your way
to what matters.

Everything that I have written, based on my reading, has a story that I can relate to some element of my lived experience. As
we approach the end of our journey through this book, there
are three more stories I'd like to share. The first is my personal
testimonial to the power of the gratitude letter.

Martin Seligman tells a story of "Gratitude Night" from his
days as a professor at the University of Pennsylvania. The assignment was for his students to bring a guest to class, someone who had been important in their lives, but to whom each
student had never offered a thanks.[50]

To complete the assignment, each student read a prepared letter of gratitude directed to their invited guest. The letters were
thoughtful, heartfelt and sincere. According to Seligman, the
evening was remarkable for many reasons—notably that every

person in the room, including students, guests, and teachers, was crying at some point.

As Seligman writes, "Crying in any class is extraordinary, and when everyone is crying, something has happened that touches the great rhizome underneath all humanity."[51]

In order to understand gratitude on the experiential level, I needed to try this exercise for myself. First, I had to think about someone who had influenced my life, but to whom I had not expressed my gratitude. I decided to thank Ian, who had served as president and CEO of Community Foundations of Canada. He'd given me a simple but powerful go-to tip, back when I was still learning how to navigate conversations during my time with the foundation.

The next step came easily because of my journal writing practice—I needed to describe with detail what Ian had done, and why his actions influenced my life. I wrote the following scene-setting preamble, which helped clear my thinking before I wrote the actual gratitude letter:

> I remember holding the telephone receiver tightly in my hand, standing at the window, looking at the parking lot below, trying to focus on your words. I was trying to quell the buzz in my brain, and it took my full effort to listen and hear what you were saying. I was having difficulty listening because I was also having difficulty being heard.
>
> I honestly don't remember what decision I was trying to make or who had initiated the call. Maybe it was another watershed moment in the life of our fledgling community foundation, because every week seemed to bring new opportunities and insurmountable roadblocks. Maybe we were

just having a chat. What I do know is that I am grateful for the numerous occasions when you took the time to listen, to hear me and to offer gentle encouragement.

You understood that being an executive director of a new organization in a small town paints a lonely landscape. Surrounded by ideas, hustle and excitement is a recipe for feeling the heavy load of responsibility defined as 'doing the right thing'.

Of course, we all want to do the right thing, but small locales have many points of connection; the overlap balanced (or imbalanced) with diversity and divergence is hard to understand when we get too myopic. You added perspective, and as I listened deeply, I gained some clarity into the possibilities, dangers and future bests that often felt misaligned. That's the reality I was living with. My job was to filter the concerns of stakeholders, community groups, donors, board members, volunteers, policymakers, legislators and bean counters. And, my job was to uphold citizenship and community values in the noise of glitz and glam that surrounds an international tourist destination which I always consider a host community first.

I remember standing alone at the window, listening to your voice. I may have been thinking about the exasperated volunteer who had recently asked me to be more decisive, confident and clear. "I don't care what you decide," he had snarled, "just make up your frigging mind."

It was true. I often did feel indecisive and uncertain. Would prospective donors, grant applicants, staff and volunteers think we were too shabby or too posh if I accepted a certain donation of furniture? Truth be told, in this instance of in-

decision, I wanted to reject a kind offer of used furniture. I really wanted to invest in practical comfort and style by spending $1,000 on a new desk and chairs. And, I didn't want to hurt anyone's feelings or be harshly judged.

Maybe you and I were talking about our upcoming spring event. You were coming to speak. We were in the friend-raising phase of our organizational development. I was certain that by carefully raising our profile, we would one day raise dollars to meet the needs of a properly furnished office. Everything was a juggling game in those days. Everything was connected, a waffle and a coin toss. Nothing could be teased apart or ignored. I had to pay very close attention to seemingly small details. You had agreed to show up, and Milly, your administrative assistant, told me that your travel expenses would be covered. "Phew!" to that, as well.

On more than one occasion, you gave me golden advice that helped me move from waffle to wisdom. This is a thank you note for helping me in a way that was significant beyond that moment, and has stayed with me for all of the years in between.

After the preamble, it was then time to write the letter, which I did during the summer of 2020. Afterwards, I sent Ian an out-of-the-blue email, requesting a Zoom call. Adhering to the instructions presented by Seligman and other gratitude researchers, I did not tell Ian why I wanted to get in touch.

When we logged on, I read my scene-setting preamble, and then read the following expression of thanks:

Dear Ian,

*A friend recently gave me a deck of **Gratitude and Soulshine** cards, and the one I am looking at right now reads "Gratitude is infusing myself with the great energy of those around me." The words remind me of conversations you and I had over the years, specifically your words, "Go where the energy is, Lorraine."*

This is a sincere note of gratitude for the gift of that expression, and for your interest and insights into my world. I remember when you visited Banff for our May 2012 event. At one point, we were walking down the stairs and you said, "I don't know what it is, but there is something special about the energy in Banff. You guys really do have something special here."

I asked, "What do you mean?" and listened to your answer. You clarified the importance of energy being an intangible vibration, and how you wanted the community foundation movement to gain momentum. You were looking for ways to pump the air in the tires of the national organization, and you had good intentions for community philanthropy then gaining traction in Canada.

Through the years, there have been many times when I was trying to figure out my simple next step, and found myself asking, "Where is the energy?" Your words, coming from beyond the waters of my mini fishbowl, helped me lift my head, look around, and consider my personal waters and my role in the world as I listened for other voices calling.

"Go where the energy is" sounds like simple advice. However, it's not so easy to filter the matrix of risks, rewards and

scenarios through the one-brain funnel of emotional energy management. To do so, one must simplify the variables, then seek direction. Where is the energy for that one next step, leading to the following one that will lead in the direction of the bigger goal?

I have used, embellished, embroidered and taken to heart the concept of energy management many times over the years. Now, when I feel the load increasing, the supports weakening, and energy lagging, I ask myself about finding new energy, and looking for lift.

What should I do? Is it physical? Emotional? Social? Should I call a friend? Go for a walk? Hit pause and go for a snooze? Gratitude has now become a vital source of energy for me. I find that being grateful gives me the lift I need. So, here is me, offering you a sincere thanks and gratitude for a coaching tip that continues to guide my thinking.

Thank you for the ways you have energized the national and international philanthropic sector with your vision and leadership. But more, to repeat myself—and from a heartfelt and personal level—thank you for taking time to listen, for being present to my concerns, offering sound advice, and giving me a positive puff of energy when my world was feeling disconnected, burdened and heavy.

Lorraine

I needed to step into the science of the gratitude letter by conducting a field test, so that I could personally validate the impact of the exercise. I'm happy to report that the conversation was a profound and emotional moment of shared experience. After a long pause, Ian replied, "Thanks, Lorraine. You really made my day. I think you may be on to something."

I was and remain passionate about the process. We were holding our respective ends of a rhizome of connection, stretched several thousand kilometers across our country, while sharing a moment of humanity. Now, it's your turn to do the same.

YOUR DAY 28 WRITING PROMPTS

1. If you were to write a gratitude letter, who might you choose to thank? Why? Check your journal notes from Day 24. What attributes of your benefactor would you highlight? What moment with them stands out in your mind?

2. Approach your inquiry from as many angles as possible as you write your scene-setting preamble. Keep in mind that your person may no longer be alive. When my *Gratitude Goes Live* group completed this exercise, one member chose to write a letter to a dear friend who had recently died. She felt better after speaking out loud about her grief, and expressing the profound gratitude she had for their friendship. It's possible that your person isn't a person at all—it could be a cherished place, a beloved pet, an heirloom, or even a special memory.

3. If you decide to complete the exercise by visiting your person, or scheduling a video conference, consider rehearsing your words. When speaking from the heart in gratitude, your voice may quiver, your hands might start to shake, and there will almost certainly be tears. But don't believe me—you need to try this for yourself.

Day 28 notes

[50]   Martin E.P. Seligman. *Authentic Happiness: Using New Positive Psychology to Realize Your Potential for Lasting Fulfillment*. United States. The Free Press, a division of Simon and Schuster, Inc. 2002. p. 72.

[51]   ibid, pg. 73.

DAY 29:

WRITING AN APOLOGY OR FORGIVENESS LETTER

Gratitude can loosen our sorrows and regrets, but we still may need to apologize.

The next story I want to relate is yet another plug for the benefits of writing in your journal. By building a good writing habit, writing letters—whether deep gratitudes or casual greetings—will become easier. This will benefit you, especially if and when it's time to write a letter of apology or forgiveness.

Gratitude can grow in small moments. One moment, you're eating a muffin, sniffing flowers, or savouring an innocent memory of crumbs on the chin of a child when suddenly feelings of gratitude well up. Writing about such times can bring a smile to your face, even on days when the crumbs have become regret or sorrow for the past.

Gazing deeply into your appreciation for things you enjoy can help you face the future with clarity, wisdom, awareness, and a new resolve to move forward, certain of the things that matter. And yet, gratitude is more than just a personal key to satisfaction.

My deepest curiosity about gratitude relates to its pro-social benefits. For years, I've wondered if gratitude can serve as a mental mindset for becoming kinder and less judgemental towards ourselves and others, and more helpful and joyful in our daily interactions.

The gratitude letter, along with sharing the letter (Day 28) is an exercise that I have *ground-truthed*. From my personal experience, plus my observations over the year of convening online gratitude groups, I can confirm that writing and sharing the letter aloud puts you directly into a field of vision from where you speak from your heart and touch the heart of another. You are being seen and heard in your deepest expression of humanity.

Writing and sharing your gratitude letter takes courage. In the middle of reading my words to Ian, I heard my voice quiver, and felt my hands begin to shake as I lost my *Zoom face* composure. At the end, it was clear that the words had touched him, but I couldn't help wonder if he thought that perhaps I was *just a bit* off my rocker in the moment of extreme vulnerability.

Seeing how gratitude can strengthen our relationships with people and things in deeply personal and powerful ways, I also needed proof that it could soften regrets and resentments.

I had never knowingly spoken to the author of the following letter, which arrived unexpectedly by email not long ago, and speaks to the power of gratitude as a bonding and healing agent. It is in reply to one of my "Rocky Mountain Outlook" columns, which I write for the local paper:

Ms. Widmer-Carson:

I have read your uplifting Outlook commentaries with interest, and believe that each commentary has an important message. I am not sure what your audience is intended to be but I hope that I may indulge myself by way of complimenting you on positive media articles. I too believe in gratitude and forgiveness in all aspects of life. I applaud what you have done in the community, and what you are continuing to do in the community.

I believe that most Banffites have a sense of community and want to serve in a way that is constructive and positive whether it be politically, or charity driven or otherwise. My intentions have always been to make Banff a better place for residents that have established roots and lived here for generations.

You are my neighbour. I live across the alley from you and walk down the path in front of your house on a regular basis. I have had pleasant exchanges with you and your husband over the years. One thing I do is to make sure to say hello to you even though we may have our differences. That is because for me it is the neighbourly thing to do and as we all know, differences between Banffites are well known and forgiveness is abundant. Over the years I have helped my neighbours and been helped by my neighbours and am extremely grateful for having good neighbours.

I apologize for anything that I have done that may have offended you personally and with that said, I hope that our good characters will be able to overcome any slight that may have occurred.

Kind Regards

***

As it turns out, the writer and I had indeed said hello in passing more than once—two fish in the same water, if you will. He had retired to our community and volunteered on some municipal committees. Shortly before his email to me, he'd been part of a letter writing campaign that challenged some of our local municipal officials to account for processes that he and his group felt were unethical. I was an observer to the campaign and had been surprised, puzzled and slightly offended by its tone and approach. I had not engaged directly, but had spoken to others about the jarring initiative. I was confused about the negative energy, and wondered aloud why this group had adopted a public *shame and blame* strategy.

The unexpected arrival of this note was proof-positive that gratitude can loosen our hearts. By writing a column and staking my ground as being grateful—along with my ongoing commitment and service to community—I received a letter of apology, once again ground-truthing the science that gratitude can soften resentment. Perhaps I did not instantly embrace the message as an apology; rather, I sat with the email and listened to my first thoughts, which were neither kind nor complimentary. However, once I began to consider the writer's courage and conviction, I felt a softening in my veneer. I subsequently wrote an honest reply, and after a few exchanges, we agreed to continue to smile at each other, say hello, and even share a few words, expressing the things for which we were grateful.

Gratitude is an energy and an underground force—a rhizome that connects us to our greater humanity. It can help us grow into our stories as heroes: courageous, tender-hearted characters with goodness in our cores.

Seeing ourselves or our neighbours in monochromatic tones of either *all good* or *all bad* diminishes the full scope of what it means to be human. We are multi-dimensional contradictions and inconsistencies—we defy one single label. Every day presents us with opportunities to be kind, vindictive, friendly, stupid, helpful, spiteful…there's no end to our human pendulum. As we express appreciation, we can at least reduce our feelings of shame, regret and guilt, and resist smearing or stereotyping our neighbours in a derogatory manner. With respect, we can paddle ahead with forward momentum and synchronous strokes.

YOUR DAY 29 WRITING PROMPTS

1. Has anyone ever apologized to you and included a gratitude as part of the apology? Have you ever apologized and been grateful in the same conversation? Do you have a regret or an apology you wish to make? Can gratitude help you find the courage to get started?

2. Write a list of five gratitudes for something special in your neighbourhood that you have been under-appreciating. It could be a dog that runs to greet you at the neighbour's fence, a cat in a window always staring out, a lush tree, flowers, or even the way moss grows out of a sidewalk crack. Expand your appreciations by writing about some of your local contradictions, starting with: *I love living in this neighbourhood because…*

DAY 30:

BHAGS AND WOOPS

Dreaming in technicolour, I used the messy method to get here. But now I know there is a scientific process for working in this field.

The last story I'd like to share relates to the final months of my work with the community foundation. Before handing in my keys, I had one more BHAG—a *Big Hairy Audacious Goal*— having to do with the basement in our building.

Where others focused on the area's dark, dank, musty atmosphere, I saw potential. Yes, it seemed a little haunted, was covered in cobwebs, and the odor was overwhelming. But, with a little imagination and a lot of positive energy, I was certain we could transform the dank into swank, more or less.

Every community needs safe gathering spaces for young people. Our town had very limited options for young adults to hang out and eat popcorn, learn about one another, and participate in age-appropriate activities while disconnecting from their mobile devices. I envisioned the basement as a welcoming, bright and cheery space where they could show up without societal pressures, and enjoy inclusive, open-hearted conversations, regardless of socio-economic status.

I called our initiative *The Spacement*, an endeavour that would increase our community's social capital, targeting young adults. After asking our inter-agency partners and stakeholders about the idea, I received mild endorsement, and continued to dream. Without any big roadblocks rising, and in consultation with an advisory committee of young adults, we sharpened our pencils and set a budget. Then, we agreed that a below-ground meeting room needed to be barrier free. We added a plan to include handrails in gender-neutral bathrooms, and incur the expense of a wheelchair lift. As one volunteer stated, "Being in a ski town means somebody always has a cast on their leg." We adjusted the plan by adding another $30,000 to the project cost, and kept dreaming.

Then came the February board meeting. In most philanthropic organizations, the volunteer board of directors holds responsibility for fiscal oversight and adherence to all legal obligations. With acceptance of the proposed budget and plan for The Spacement—the total came out to $150,000—the project could kick into high gear. I would run toward my finish line like a horse heading out to a spring pasture.

During the board meeting, I had to admit that my plan for raising revenue was not secure, and no, the dollars were not sitting in our current bank account. However, with the board behind me—and with their expression of trust confirming that the work aligned with our mandate and mission—I was confident we could raise the cash.

When I presented the details, there was no question that I was basing my projections on a mix of intuition, understanding of the local landscape, and our organization's relationships with various partners. During the meeting, one of the newer board members asked me directly, "Can you please explain how you plan to raise the money?"

Even though he was polite, I was flabbergasted. I had to fight with every bone in my body to avoid saying something pithy to the tune of "Trust me, I know what I am doing."

The thing is, in that moment, trust was the very thing missing. To the volunteer's credit, he didn't know me, and had only recently moved to town. We had no shared experience through which to build trust. With no prior working relationship, the initiative I was presenting was, in effect, a dream. And, as BHAGs go, the farther the stretch, the larger the risks.

I took a deep breath and explained where we stood in each of several fundraising-related conversations. A number of individual and corporate donors had expressed interest, we'd launched a letter campaign, and we had been executing a community engagement plan for months. With timid confidence, I explained that an application for $50,000 was sitting on the desk of a major funder who had supported us in the past, and who liked our work. My sixth sense told me that The Spacement would align with the mandate of that particular grant-maker, but the process still needed to unfold. Sadly, on the evening I presented the budget, I lacked both the cash and commitment that would have made the dream sound promising.

In the end, the board offered tentative approval for the project, with conditions, of course. I should have been thrilled. Instead, what stuck with me was how flushed my cheeks had gotten at the sting of being second-guessed.

Walking out of the board room, I confided in Carsten, a senior board member, that I felt the wind had been taken out of my sails. In fact, I told him I was disappointed that the conversation had been so difficult. Carsten and I had worked together for several years. He smiled at me, adding, "Well, if I hadn't worked with and watched you for this many years, I would probably have asked the same questions. I thought the conversation was a good one." Point well taken.

A week later, I was sitting with Bill, the chair of the board of directors. In less than four months, I would conclude this chapter of my working career. I was certain that The Spacement would fill a community need, but knew that further delay would mean deferring the project to the incoming leadership team, which carried the risk of losing it altogether. I was in a BHAG hurry, and time was not on my side.

As Bill and I reviewed our options, the phone rang unexpectedly. It was early evening, and I excused myself as I took the call. On the other end was the funder I'd been waiting to hear from. "Our committee just met about The Spacement project," he said. "You've been approved for the full amount of $50,000. I will start the paperwork tomorrow, and we will get the cheque processed shortly."

What happened next was nothing short of happy dancing. The flood of relief, gratitude and joy at hearing those words still produces a kind of euphoria when I think about it. Bill and I high-fived each other as I whooped and smiled unabashedly—all worry, concern and internal second-guesses were silenced.

The gratitude-filling work of helping our community still warms my heart. Gratitude and its pro-social benefits were core to our organizational culture. Our staff, donors, volunteers, event organizers, managers, funders and even the universe conspired to co-create and help execute on this—one more strand to a vision of a smarter, kinder and more caring community.

At every level of life, trust can alleviate fears, and help us feel supported and connected. Trusting our partners can increase our ability to do more, and with greater efficiency. Without trust, litigation is a constant threat, and plans can become too safe, a bit stale and relatively uninspired. Without the support of trusted scaffolding, falls and mishaps can dint a dream beyond repair. In an environment of mistrust and risk-aversion, we may not even trust ourselves to dream big.

It takes work and positive energy to move in the direction of your dreams. With *laddership* that is grounded in trust, gratitude, positivity and possibility, dreams can happen. When trust is given, whether in the form of money, social currency, friendship or belief, it is a rare and precious gift. In such special moments, magic happens.

YOUR DAY 30 WRITING PROMPTS

1. Have you ever dreamed a BIG dream? Were you able to bring it into the light of day? Do you permit yourself to have flights of fancy and dream in technicolour?

2. My messy and risky methodology worked, in part because our organization had credibility among people at the street level, or *street cred* as one board member called it. What type or level of street cred is connected to your big dream? How can you step into your credibility with confidence?

3. Here, at our Day 30 end station, I want to leave you with one last technique, as recommended by researchers. It is called WOOP—not a loud exuberant shout of joy, but a four-step thought exercise that can take you from dream to outstanding results.

    The methodology and rationale are outlined in the book, *Rethinking Positive Thinking*, which I highly recommend. The book's author, Dr. Gabrielle Oettingen, explains the science behind encouraging ourselves to reach positive fantasies with optimism, motivating ourselves for success and satisfaction.[52] You may also want to check out the website, woopmylife.org for more inspiration.

Here are a few steps to turn WOOP thinking into today's writing prompt:

- Set your idea, goal or intention firmly and vividly in your mind. Really dream it into reality. Consider this the Wish.
- Keep dreaming about the Opportunities (or Outcomes, if you like) that will unfold when it is realized. This is your *dreaming in technicolour* phase, and it holds the energy for days when things go sideways.
- Now think about the Obstacles. Don't be afraid to lean on your years of experience, the wisdom of your many minds, friends or partners, or even some nay-sayers who can help you understand your Obstacles. This step contrasts your desired Opportunities/Outcomes, complete with pitfalls, helping you anticipate the space between you and success.
- Finally, begin to write out your Plan. Just like athletes at the starting line: get ready, set—go!

4. Wrap up with five reasons to be grateful today. Here's my list of five from the days of The Spacement initiative:

- Members of the board of directors were confident enough to influence each other to trust me. Some members may have even been asked to take a leap of faith that felt a bit uncomfortable.
- My BHAG was embellished, embroidered and supported by people with gifts of time, talent and money. Others were willing to dream along with me through my messy and iterative processes. Our organization needed to take the initiative and do most of the heavy lifting to get things started,

but others were willing to nudge, push and pull us along. I'm not sure—community leadership, or laddership?

- The trust and support of others in community—individuals, donors, agency partners, and workmates—helped me believe that the dream was worth dreaming.

- Happily, two donors leveraged their resources with a shared commitment to projects that focused on wheelchair accessibility. With this investment, the wheelchair lift was installed, and the dream, now a three-way shared vision, became barrier-free.

- The phone call that the big grant had landed came at just the right moment. With the news, the wisdom of Greek philosopher Cicero was affirmed: "Gratitude is not only the greatest of the virtues, but the parent of all others." To which I say, "Hallelujah and Amen!"

Now it's your turn to WOOP.

Day 30 notes

[52] Gabriele Oettingen. *Rethinking Positive Thinking: Inside the New Science of Motivation*. United States. Penguin Random House LLC. 2015. pp. 79, 134-135.

AFTERWORD

The problem with simplifying any system that's full of variables is that we risk focusing on one *special* thing or goal, whether it is to be happy, fit, trim, healthy, self-sufficient, win the race, what have you. We soon learn that it is *never* about just one thing, but the myriad of things we discover along the way. With that said, it is my tentative assertion that gratitude may be *the single thing* that can hold the door open to every goal in the unfolding story of your life.

John Muir, often referred to as the Founding Father of America's National Parks system, wrote "When we try to pick out anything by itself, we find it hitched to everything else in the universe." [53] As you have gone along, paying attention, looking for reasons to be grateful, chances are that you have found some interconnections and relationships that were hitched to things you hadn't previously considered. Plus, your writing has likely given you more ideas about what matters. Not sure? Skip to pages 182 and 184, and review the gratitude gauge and accountability list you completed during the early days of your journey. What's changed for you? Why not complete these two exercises again, now that you've grown your practice, and note your changes?

There's a good chance that the connections between your mindset on any given day, your personal realities (everything from household chores, to minor inconveniences, to your workload), your *big rocks*, memories, and the trajectory you envision for yourself have all come under scrutiny. Has the experience been interesting? Upsetting? Thought-provoking? As you have worked your way through these exercises with a pen and your journal, I hope you have stayed kind and gentle with yourself. And, I hope that you have continued to pose and follow the threads of questions as they've come. After all, as humans, we are curious by nature, and our curiosity—the willingness to ask questions and seek answers—helps us grow.

Now, I need to return to lake ecology, and add some notes to my Day 9 entry.

As a naïve and wide-eyed 21-year-old university graduate, I was fascinated to learn about the critical role that a lake's sediments play in its ecology. The bottom layer (the benthic layer) is a mysterious system of processes that ultimately determines a lake's state of health. It is a vital interface between the water column that lies above, and the layers of bottom sludge; a convergence of life, seasons and history in real time.

In the here and now, a lake in Canada has a summer season for growing and producing, and a winter season during which death and decay are the primary cycles. In every season, the bacteria, bugs, fish, amoebas, plankton and algae chew on the flotsam and jetsam that enter the system. As the processes unfold, nutrients such as oxygen, carbon and nitrogen are either added or taken away. In the great exchange of life, the creatures in the sediments are critical in determining everything that matters in the health and existence of that lake. The nutrient load can be manageable, and the system can cope with the given dynamics; or, a load may be toxic, meaning too much of one thing in too short a time. For instance, a toxic shock of too much sewage, industrial waste or even bird poop can shift the balance, putting the lake's ecology into serious flux.

The quality of the bottom sludge of a lake is considered an important indicator of a lake's health and vitality. The same is true with human *beans* and our personal ecology. If you are part of a culture that embraces the strengths of writing in a journal and noting your reasons to be grateful, you are better equipped to dredge through the sediments of your soul and find buried treasures.

Much has been written about the lessons we can learn from our mistakes—*teachable moments*, if you will. Mistakes can be good or bad—but every mistake is a lesson if we care to listen and learn. In my life, I have often said that the most difficult lessons are likely the ones I needed most.

Every good system, process or relationship needs to consider how to manage miscalculations and left-overs—those parts in a system that can help us recycle, repurpose, recalibrate and keep going. In his book, *Outliers*, Malcolm Gladwell introduces us to "The Story of Success," and the 10,000 hour rule. No matter the exact number, reaching a point of mastery or expertise requires long hours of practice.[54] In essence, by practicing, rehearsing, falling down and getting up again, as you work hard for 10,000 hours at your craft, you will arrive at mastery, and gain the right mix of self-confidence and humility to consider yourself at a certain level of proficiency and expertise.

Until we reach that higher place of mastery, we need to keep thinking, processing, learning, occasionally failing, but always growing. It takes energy, time, patience, and plenty of curiosity for the good stuff to emerge. So, stay patient and show kindness toward yourself and others. I wish them both for you.

Afterword Notes

[53]   John Muir. *My First Summer in the Sierra*. United States. Houghton Mifflin. 1911. p. 110. Borrowed and shared from https://vault.sierraclub.org/john_muir_exhibit/writings/misquotes.aspx.

[54]   Malcolm Gladwell. "The 10,000 Hour Rule," in *Outliers: The Story of Success*. Canada. Penguin Books, 2009. pp. 35 – 68.

ACKNOWLEDGMENTS

As our family has grown together and apart; as the stories of family, friends, teammates, and neighbours have risen and plummeted; as time has moved on; as our community of communities has won, lost, advanced, and retreated, it is obvious that growth, decline and change are constant. As my birth family and friends have faced successes, defeats, declines, illnesses and addictions, made mistakes, and been lost to the ravages of suicide, my journal has helped me process life's events. Perhaps the greatest strength is to stay humble, and to keep striving to do good without letting anyone know.

Gratitude is a key strength that can soften some of our regret, encourage forgiveness, and help us move closer to accepting truths—even those that began as lies. With gratitude and time, I hope that we can raise our social and cultural levels of trust, empathy, kindness and equity. We need a paradigm shift in the direction of greater cooperation, humility, kindness and courage. We need to find new ways for working together. I acknowledge my obliviousness to some people's lives, and I am willing to commit and recommit to an idea that shines a light on a brighter future for all.

At this moment, I want to acknowledge some of the people who have helped me stay with this project, to keep writing, and to commit with grit and belief that there was something in the sediment of my soul that needed saying.

Thanks to all of the writers, thought leaders, research assistants, community advocates and health care providers, including a few very talented orthopedic surgeons, physiotherapists, nurses and administrators, who have helped our family regain mobility and agility, and to come back stronger. Canada's health care system is doing its best to manage the challenges of COVID, cut-backs, expectations and realities, and remains essential to our collective health and well-being.

To the scientists, researchers, ground-truthers and field workers who are collecting the stories and field notes: thank you for calibrating and helping us understand the relationship between theory and reality. Also, thanks to all of the honest messengers and truth-seekers who understand that nature and culture are critical elements to every place. And, to those who carry wisdom and words that can never be wound into a small tight ball that brings higher understanding—thank you.

To my beta readers and curious cheerleaders who politely did not ask why my writing project was taking me so long. Thanks go to Connie, Colleen, Helen, Colin, Nancy, Gordon, Shirley, Donna, Mona and Lindsay, for your gentle encouragement and permission to keep trying.

To friends who invited me to coffee or to ski, even when I kept declining because I was writing—thank you! To writing coaches and workshop co-ordinators who have encouraged my writing process over the years, thank you.

I want to acknowledge the support of many other colleagues and coaches who have helped me move forward with these ideas, even when I did not quite know where the road was leading. And to my special and dear friend Jane who is exemplary in many ways, not the least of which is an honest assessment of my soul's deepest soil, who said to me in February 2020: "You have no idea what this will become." She then paused, and added with a mischievous smile, that ever-important word, "yet." I hope that everyone has a solid friend like Jane—one who holds up mirrors both wondrous and humbling.

Thanks to my 2020 Zoom gratitude group participants—you helped me ground-truth the science over the course of a year, adding real-life experience and authentic evidence to my field study. In a series of amazingly insightful conversations and moments of delight, during the season of COVID chaos, we took leaps of faith, navigated technological challenges, and grounded ourselves around the topic of gratitude and its transformative power. Thank you for showing up, opening your hearts and minds, and sharing so honestly.

More recently, I have benefited from the talent of two other fellow travellers. Thanks to Lieve Maas of Bright Lights Design, and writer/editor Dave Jarecki. You both nudged me along, and helped this book follow its own journey toward completion. Thank you. Some days, the process felt like I was stumbling in the mud, trying to read the map with a penlight and a broken pair of eyeglasses. Then the sun came up, the needle shifted, and the muses, energy, and good vibrations brought inspiration—and we kept going.

Finally, thank you, Dear Universe, for delivering into our home the gifts of our beautiful children: Philip, Matthew, Angela and Heidi, standing shoulder to shoulder with Erwin, my fellow star-gazer. And now, our next generation of ski racers are bursting out of the gates with Louis-Pierre and Uncle Keith encouraging Evia and Florina to bend their knees and ankles.

And to you, Dear Reader: thank you for taking me along on *your* journey. Now that you know what you know, what are you thinking? What are the things that need to change as you ensure that your life and legacy move you closer to your next set of goals and personal bests?

October 10, 2021.

APPENDIX

GRATITUDE GAUGE:

COMPLETE THIS QUIZ AS YOU BEGIN DAY 1, THEN AGAIN AFTER DAY 30

You've heard that gratitude is a good thing, but how do you go from knowing it's good to showing it and growing it? Are you grateful but not sure how to start? Ready to nudge your gratitude-gauge from minimal to more? This quiz will help you benchmark your starting point.

Respond to the following and rate yourself using the scale:

1. Never   **4. Pretty much true**

2. Occasionally   **5. Yes. Absolutely. Always.**

3. Neutral

Every day I take time to savour something special – a taste, sound, smell…	Score: _____
I make a written list of my Gratitudes every single day	Score: _____
I always say "Thank you" – even for the smallest thing	Score: _____
When I look back, I know I have been richly blessed in my life	Score: _____
When I am outside or go for a walk, I always notice something amazing	Score: _____

For these next statements, rate yourself using the scale:

1. Completely true   **4. Not really**

2. Mostly true   **5. No, not true at all**

3. Neutral

To be honest, my days are just too busy to   Score: _____
count my blessings

If I had to list the things in life that I am   Score: _____
grateful for, my list would be very short

My successes and achievements are primarily   Score: _____
due to my individual efforts and personal
strengths, not because of the support of others

TOTAL GRATITUDE SCORE =/40

About your score:

Less than 20 – Gratitude may not be your greatest personal strength and that's okay. As the saying goes, the best time to plant a tree was 20 years ago. The second best time? Today.

20 and higher – Great! You are incorporating gratitude

Commit to tracking your joys every day for the next two weeks. After that, track your gratitudes three times a week for the next few weeks. Adjust as it makes sense for you.

As you continue strengthening your muscles, pay careful attention and notice: Did anything special happen today? Start looking for tiny happy thoughts, or times you chuckled.

GRATITUDE ACCOUNTABILITY LIST:

TO COMPLETE AFTER DAY 8

You know that gratitude is a good thing, and you are ready to commit to a better gratitude habit, but you know that cultivating a new habit takes intentional effort. Use this list to check in and make notes. You are your own personal trainer. As you get ready, use this list to add a level of professionalism and accountability for your effort. In the days to come, when the going gets tough and the time is hard to find, refer to this list and recommit, recalibrate and re-energize your efforts.

1. What a good gratitude practice means to me:
    _____

2. I would like to get more gratitude into my life because I want to:

    *   Feel less anxious, be more positive
    *   Sleep better
    *   Have more energy – physical, emotional, social, spiritual
    *   Be more hopeful and optimistic
    *   Reconsider my sense of purpose and meaning in life
    *   Feel healthier
    *   Get along better with others – friends, family, colleagues
    *   Make a decision about _____ (something that is coming up)
    *   Other: _____

3. My starting date is/was: _____.

4. Today is Day 8. Date: _____ My options include deciding if I want to:

   - Give up completely
   - Put this habit on the calendar and start on another date: _____
   - Continue every day for the next 20 days
     End date: _____
   - Schedule this habit for twice a week, for 10 weeks
     End date: _____
   - Other: _____

5. I also understand that this is not meant to be a stressful activity, but a chance to take a pause, look inward, look upward and outward and set some realistic expectations for myself. I understand that:

   - This commitment will cost me about 30 minutes a day.
   - I am the boss of me. This is a personal practice and I will give myself permission to modify in ways that suit my personality, my personal circumstances and preferences.
   - If others ask, I will tell them that I am exploring the benefits of a new habit, and will tell them about it when I have figured out some things, or when I feel ready.
   - I may need to manage my time and energy differently. This may include giving up or changing some habits related to social media, hobbies, physical or social activities.

6. Each day that I write in my journal, I will:

    - Write with a pen that fits my hand and that moves easily across the page.
    - Customize my journal so that it is inviting, appealing, suits my personality and makes me feel good.
    - Find a private place and focus on the task at hand.
    - Find a flat surface, seated at a desk in a chair while writing.
    - Recognize my best time of day. First thing in the morning? Last thing before bed?
    - What else? _____

7. Another commitment to myself:

I will try my best to develop a habit for writing in my journal and tracking my gratitudes on a regular basis. I also realize that writing in a journal is one way, may even be the best way, according to the science, but my way will be a mix-n-match exercise that includes:

- Writing lists
- Keeping a gratitude jar
- Taking photos and diarizing
- Write thank you notes and gratitude letters
- Putting stickie notes on sweet things
- Sketching, painting, drawing
- Collecting quotes and photos
- Making a scrapbook
- Using digital tools, including voice memos and/or e-notes for tracking
- Posting to social media
- Intentionally noting my joys as I meditate, pray or reflect in private

- Talking to myself, and taking inventory of my body, mind and energy
- Having intentional conversations with others
- Other _____

8. I promise to be gentle with myself, and to use positive self-talk—most of the time. Rather than get overwhelmed, I will organize my thoughts in 4-D:

   ✓ Do today – urgent and a top priority
   ✓ Delay – put it on the calendar for a future date
   ✓ Defer – ask for help and decide who that will be
   ✓ Delete – clear it from my list of priorities and feel good about being decisive

9. More notes to self: _____

My signature: _____

ADDING SOME SOUL
TO YOUR VALUES:
REVIEW AND COMPLETE
AFTER DAY 23

What PERSONAL VALUES are of the greatest importance to you at this time in your life? Think about your values in terms of your associational community of communities, the compass points that guide your life work. Consider the following list, which I've adopted from The Legacy Questionnaire in *Values-Based Estate Planning* by Scott C. Fithian: [55]

- **Philanthropic, Civic values** such as community involvement, service to others, gifts of time, sharing skills, donating money — Score: __

- **Economic, Financial values** such as financial planning, managing material possessions, caring for built assets, money — Score: __

- **Spiritual values** such as inner growth, meditation, faith activities, sacred commitments — Score: __

- **Work values** such as effort, energy, training, building competence, professional achievement — Score: __

- **Physical, Recreational values** such as sports, leisure, personal care, relaxation, exercise — Score: __

- **Cultural values** such as music, visual arts, travel, reading, writing, photography — Score: __

- **Relational values** such as family, friends, neighbours, romantic partners, work associates, your pet(s) — Score: __

- **Educational values** such as study, self-improvement, academic achievement — Score: __

- **Other** (specify) _____ — Score: __

Now, think about how you invest your time, energy and money on a weekly or monthly basis. Give yourself a score for each value where "0" means you spend no time or energy, and "10" means you spend a great deal of your time and personal resources.

If your values are your motivation, and time is one of your most precious commodities, are you happy with your scores? Do you want to pay more or less attention to any of these values?

Fithian also poses the legacy question, "To whom do you feel a sense of obligation, when it comes to the distribution of your wealth?" The list of options includes: spouse, parents, grandparents, children, step-children, employees, a higher power, mentor, friends…what do you say? Make a list of gratitudes for the people, places and things that make your life worth living. Refer to this list when considering any big decisions related to life, legacy, and how you want to be remembered.

Adding Some Soul Notes

[55] Scott. C. Fithian, *Values-Based Estate Planning: A Step-by-Step Approach to Wealth Transfer for Professional Advisors.* United States: John Wiley & Sons, Inc. 2002. p 204.

ABOUT THE AUTHOR

In the summer of 1976, Lorraine Widmer-Carson landed her first Banff job as a chamber maid, then as a waitress. She even found a place to live, which felt very lucky. Between 1980 and 2017, she worked for Parks Canada, the Whyte Museum, The Friends of Banff National Park, The Banff Centre, and ended her career in community as executive director of the Banff Canmore Community Foundation. She and her Swiss-Canadian husband, four children and ever-expanding circles of family and friends have been hiking, skiing, exploring and adoring the Canadian Rockies, while also running Ticino Swiss-Italian Restaurant, since 1979.

Lorraine believes that gratitude is one of life's golden through-threads that can guide how we process information and influence our habits of mind. "From unconscious to conscious, from deeply personal to universal and soul-shakingly wonderful, gratitude is a life skill and a social skill. Gratitude can help us reframe our memories and help us breathe more contentedly as we commit and recommit to nudging the needle towards positive change, motivating ourselves to try to do it just a little bit better, next time."

An Ecology of Gratitude: Writing Your Way to What Matters is her first book. Learn more about Lorraine and her work at www.grassrootsgratitude.ca.

Made in the USA
Columbia, SC
16 November 2021

49094600R00107